FINANCIAL PLANNING FOR COLLEGE GRADUATES

A step-by-step guide for the first five years
of your career, and beyond.

ANDREW C. SCHAFFER, J.D., M.B.A

PRESS

Financial Planning for College Graduates
A step-by-step guide for the first five years of your career, and beyond.
by Andrew C. Schaffer, J.D., M.B.A.

Printed in the United States of America.
Edited by Xulon Press.

ISBN 9781498477284

www.xulonpress.com

Dedicated to my wife, Elizabeth, and our two daughters, Lydia and Lila, who have immeasurably enriched my life in every way.

About the author

Andrew C. Schaffer, J.D., M.B.A. is a full-time Professor of Finance and Law at Dallas Baptist University. He has taught financial planning, insurance and investments for over 20 years at the university level. Prior to joining academia, Dr. Schaffer worked as a tax attorney and investment specialist for clients of a worldwide accounting firm and two investment companies. Areas of expertise include retirement planning and distributions and investments. He earned his law degree and Master of Business Administration from Texas Tech University. He earned a Bachelor of Business Administration (B.B.A.) from Baylor University with a dual major in Finance and Financial Services. He has held investment licenses, including Series 7, Series 63 and Group 1 licenses. In his spare time, he enjoys traveling to coastal regions and taking cruises with his family.

Table of Contents

Part IV: Saving and Investing

Part V: Other Topics

Part VI: The Years Ahead

Preface

This book is designed for people who are about to graduate from college or who have recently graduated. My intent is to provide easy to follow, sound financial advice for these college students and graduates. I have written this book for all college graduates, regardless of their major. No background or degree in business or related fields is needed. My goal is for current and former students to start building their financial futures on solid ground immediately, so that they will have more secure lives later.

I have taught financial planning for over 20 years to undergraduates and as of this writing my wife and I have put two girls through college. Perhaps my next book will be about how in the world to afford tuition! However, the purpose of this book is to provide basic financial guidance to the age group with whom I interact in my job as a professor every day – twenty-something year old college students!

One of the things that continually surprises me is the lack of financial knowledge people in their 20's have. Despite the wealth of information (pun intended) available at their fingertips via smartphones and the internet, most students have very little real understanding of subjects such as budgeting, debt, credit cards, identity theft, compound interest, investments, insurance, employee benefits, taxes, or retirement plans. Some students, of course, do have some expertise in one or more of these areas, but most do not. My goal in writing this book is to guide current and recent college students step-by-step, through the financial planning process, so that they can start on the road to financial independence and improve their financial standing over time.

Sometimes, we can glean wisdom, including financial wisdom, from unexpected sources. A nutritionist recently visited my campus, and she had some insights related to dieting…but as I listened to her, I realized many of her points apply to personal finance as well. Here were some of her ideas:

-   Dieting is not about deprivation.
-   Losing weight is about liberation through moderation.
-   Many diet books promise fast results with gimmicky or unproven ideas or false promises.

Each of these applies to personal finance. This book is not about depriving you of enjoying life, or some of your income. Yes, it takes some discipline to succeed financially, but you do not have to rearrange your life to do so.

Also, this book is about liberation (freedom!!) from financial stress through moderation. This means that moderate actions, both financially and otherwise, can result in outsized success – over the long-term. Moderation also means you are more likely to succeed since the odds of having success by living a solid life financially consistently are much higher than via a get-rich quick scheme.

Finally, I do not make false promises in this book. Just as moderate exercise enhances health over decades, living out the principles in this book should provide guidance to build wealth and decrease debt over the long-term.

I have written this book with our two daughters in mind. One is a business major and the other is not. They have busy schedules and that will not stop after they graduate and begin careers. So, I have written this book to be an easily readable guide.

Each chapter will contain an introduction to a different financial topic. Most chapters also contain at least one Action Item – something the reader should do immediately to address the financial issue in the chapter. Each Action Item is also meant to guide the reader in a short amount of time. If a student or graduate is single, or recently married, and the subject demands different instructions for each, I will provide that as well.

Finally, don't feel like you have to do everything in this book at once. Consider it a step-by-step guide. Utilize the information in this book on a weekly or monthly basis as needed. Apply the information in one or two chapters each month, for instance, or as the subject comes up in your life.

One key thing I stress to my students is that financial planning is a <u>process</u>, not a one-time event. The most important thing is to <u>implement</u> the information in this book. **The biggest single obstacle to financial success is procrastination.** I hope you will use the information in this book not just this week or this month, but each year ahead. So, let's begin!

PART I: GETTING STARTED

Chapter 1

Where Am I?

"Where you are going is more important than where you are."

When I was a teenager my youth minister once told us, "Where you are going is more important than where you are." What he meant was that regardless of where we found ourselves at the moment, we could build our relationship with God daily, and thus head in the right direction. I have always remembered that phrase, because it applies to so many things. It applies not just spiritually but also personally and financially. Whether you come from a wealthy background, a middle-class background, or a background of relative poverty, you can build your life and your future with good planning and good choices. Certainly getting a college degree is one of those good choices! Planning your financial future by reading this book is another one. Note that the phrase "Where you are going is more important than where you are" implies that you know where you are right now. Most people have no idea where they are financially. Your first step, then, is to find that out. Ask yourself these questions:

Have you ever run out of money before the end of the month?

Have you ever wondered: "Where in the world did all the money go?"

We can find answers to this using a tool called Cash Management.

Cash management first requires knowing where you are right now. The way to find that out is to track <u>and</u> <u>categorize</u> the monthly expenses you have, and subtract those from your monthly income. Your first step to financial success is to categorize every expense over a month, and then add each category up at the end of the month. This way, you will know, for instance, how much you spent eating out, how much you spent on clothes, and gasoline, etc.

In many ways, this is the hardest part of your financial plan in the whole book. The reason is that it takes some time, and some record keeping. Remember, it is only for one month.

As you do this during the month, here is a key phrase I want you to remember:

Financial success is as much about discipline as it is about money.

As you track everything, I want you to list and categorize every single expense. Be as specific as possible in categorizing expenses. Try to minimize listing items as "miscellaneous."

To make this easier, feel free to round expenses up or down to the nearest dollar. For instance, if you buy a cup of coffee one morning for $4.29, you can round that expense down to $4.00 and categorize it as 'eating out' or 'restaurant', or 'Starbucks' if that is a common habit. If you buy groceries for $128.64, you can round that up to $129.00 and categorize it as 'groceries.'

One critical thing to know is that it is important to record and categorize even small expenses: Just three dollars each day for a snack at work equals almost $1,000 per year!

Here are some sample categories of expenses to help you get started:

Rent or Mortgage payment

Groceries

Phone (home, cell, data charges)

Eating Out

Haircut

Electric Bill

Water Bill

Gas Bill for apartment or house

Tithe

Car payment(s)

Car repair or maintenance

Gasoline

Auto insurance premium

Health insurance premium

Life insurance premium

Gifts

Clothes

Entertainment

Subscriptions (online and/or paper)

Dry cleaning

Student loan payment(s)

School-related expenses (children or graduate school)

Child care

Credit card payments for prior charges (We will talk about debt management in an upcoming chapter.)

Miscellaneous

Feel free to add your own categories.

There are significant benefits of tracking your expenses in the exercise above. First, you will be able to answer the two questions I mentioned above:

Where did all of the money go?

What caused us to run out before the end of the month?

Many people are surprised that they are spending so much in one or two areas, such as eating out or buying clothes.

The second benefit is now you can gain control over your expenses, because you know where your money is going each month.

Once you complete tracking all your expenses during a month's period, add up all the expenses in each category, and subtract them from your take-home pay each month. Here is an example:

Suppose Dave earns $66,000 per year, and is paid once a month. His gross pay each month is: $66,000 / 12 months = $5,500.00. However, income taxes, F.I.C.A. (Social Security and Medicare taxes), and other expenses in this example (such as healthcare premiums) are also taken out of Dave's pay-check, leaving him with $3,400.00 that is deposited into his checking account each month.

In this example, Dave should now subtract all his monthly expenses from the $3,400.00 so he can see how his expenses compare with his income.

Here is how Dave's income and expenses might look:

Take Home Pay	$3,400.00
Rent	$ 750.00
Groceries	$ 425.00
Phone & Internet (cell, data charges, etc.)	$ 80.00
Eating Out	$ 367.00
Haircut	$ 30.00
Electric Bill	$ 85.00
Water Bill	$ 55.00
Gas Bill for apartment	$ 60.00
Tithe	$ 200.00
Car payment(s)	$ 460.00
Car repair or maintenance	$ 0.00
Gasoline	$ 115.00
Auto insurance premium	$ 92.00
Health insurance premium	$ 118.00
Life insurance premium	$ 0.00
Gifts	$ 71.00
Clothes	$ 243.00
Entertainment	$ 77.00
Subscriptions (online and/or paper)	$ 22.00
Dry cleaning	$ 34.00
Student loan payment(s)	$ 390.00
School-related expenses	$ 0.00
Child care	$ 0.00
Credit card payments for prior charges	$ 250.00
Miscellaneous	$ 45.00
Total Expenses	$3,969.00
Take Home Pay Minus Expenses	$(549.00)

At first glance, it looks like Dave is spending $549.00 more each month than he is earning. However, note that Health Insurance in the amount of $118.00 was subtracted out of Dave's paycheck before his net pay. Since it was already taken out, Dave can 'add back' that $118.00 ...since it was already deducted from his paycheck. Thus, in this example, he is spending $431.00 more each month than he is earning. This is very valuable information. Now that Dave knows this, he can use it to adjust his spending. He would not have known he was spending $431 more than he was earning if he had not tracked his expenses for a month. He also would not have known where all his money went. In Dave's case, he spent $367 eating out, and $243 on clothes. He could probably cut back some in each of those areas, and live on what he is earning.

The Next Step Is To Develop A Budget.

After tracking your expenses for a month, take a look at the total of each category of your expenses, and see if you spent more than you planned or realized. If you did, try to cut back on some expenses so that you can save some money. Also, plan to spend a certain amount in each category each month. This sounds really hard at first…but realize that most categories will not vary tremendously month-to-month. Categories such as 'restaurant' and 'clothes' and 'entertainment' can vary a great deal each month. Other spending categories, such as 'groceries' and 'gasoline' are usually closer in amount from month-to-month.

One challenge with budgeting is that it implies constraint. People usually don't like to feel constrained. If something is too big of a life-changer, most people simply will not do it very long. But I have an idea to help you stick with a budget long-term, so that you will be successful!

Build in some 'Mad Money' into your monthly budget. This could be $100, or $200 or $300 or so.

This is an extra amount that you can set aside to splurge – you can spend this each month on some special item or event, such as a special night out, or some nice clothes, or whatever you want to do. This way, you don't lose the ability to enjoy your life, and you can still control your expenses. Of course, this needs to be a reasonable amount of money, so you can still spend less than you earn each month.

Many people in their 20's spend more than they earn, and they intuitively know it. In fact, an article in 2014 in the Wall Street Journal titled 'For Young, a Savings Deficit' by Josh Zumbrun pointed out that Americans under the age of 35 actually have a *negative* savings rate of about 2% per year. This means they are either taking on additional debt or withdrawing money (or both) but are saving nothing. This example is a core reason I am writing this book…I do not want you to be in that position. The tools in this chapter will help you avoid this!

I know it is not easy to spend less than you earn…and it is hard to save money. So far, this chapter has been about Income and Expenses. But what if you thought about…

Income and *Expectations*

Most people think "I'd be able to save more if I just made a little more money".

What do you think you would do if your income doubled? Would your expenses remain the same?

Would you stay in the same house or apartment?

Would you drive the same cars?

Would you keep the same clothes, take the same vacations, etc.?

Most of us would not. Most of the time as our income increases, our expenses increase as well. But this is actually really good news for you.

Here is the reason why:

> Most people blame their lack of saving money on a lack of income…we can rationalize the fact that we have only a limited control over the amount we earn.

> However, you and I have a greater ability to control how much we spend. Most spending is a choice – how nice of a place you live in, how much you spend on a car, how much you spend eating out, etc. Since a lot of spending is in your control, you should be able to save money over time, especially as your income increases.

> Over time, incomes tend to increase. If you choose to keep your expenses relatively stable, you should be able to save some money for a house, another car, retirement, etc.

> One of my former students, Vince Kelly, uses a web site to help him with budgeting. It is: youneedabudget.com.

After looking at it, I am intrigued by it. One of the main things it helps people do is get to a point that they are budgeting one month ahead. This means that people get to a point that they have a savings account equal to one month's expenses and build on that, so that they are not living paycheck-to-paycheck anymore.

Action Items for this chapter:
1. **Track and categorize one month's worth of expenses.**
2. **Using that, create a budget that allows you to spend less than you earn.**
3. **Build in some 'Mad Money' into the budget so you can enjoy life and still spend less than you earn!**
4. **Consider using youneedabudget.com**

Chapter 2

Ready, Set, GOAL!

"Where there is no vision, the people perish." Proverbs 29:18 (KJV)

The prior chapter was about finding out where you stand financially. This chapter is about setting and reaching goals, now that you have an idea how you are doing financially. This book is about financial planning for people in their 20's. But it is also about hope! What do you hope for? What do you want to accomplish? Are you worried about your prospects in our economy? What are your goals? Without goals, there is no direction. Without vision (hope) the people perish.

A common saying in the financial planning business is that people don't plan to fail – they fail to plan. There is considerable truth to that statement. Most people do not know where they are financially because they do not want to know. Many times people have a vague sense they are not doing things quite right. For instance, most people know they are not saving enough money. Many people know they are too heavily in debt. But most of us do not really want to think about it. The good news is that there are ways of addressing all of these problems.

It is sometimes tempting for people in their 20's to assume that they do not need to worry about personal finances yet. But I have taught finance for over 20 years, and I cannot tell you the number of people I have taught in their 30's, 40's, and 50's who have said to me "I wish I had taken your financial planning course when I was younger, because I would be so much better off now." So as you take this read this book, dive in and learn the information, and most of all, apply it <u>now</u> for your future!

One key phrase I mentioned before is: **Financial planning is as much about discipline as it is about money.**

Here is a second key phrase: **The single biggest obstacle to financial success is procrastination.**

People put off financial planning and then just live week-to-week and month-to-month. They then find themselves with little savings in their 30's, 40's and 50's.

So, don't put any of this off! Your first step was to create a budget. Step #2 is to set goals. Goal setting might seem easy but is actually a vital step in this financial planning process. Many times people do not know what their goals are or what they should be. In the case of a couple each person may have different goals or priorities. I will address that below.

Goals can be short-term, intermediate term, or long-term. Short-term goals are those goals can be completed in one year or less. Intermediate term goals should be able to be met within about five years, and long-term goals are those that are longer than five years out.

Goals should also be clear. Many times, people list goals that are more like wishes than actual goals. For instance, someone might say, "I want to be rich someday." And that is nice. While a lot of people might express that, few will reach it, because that is just a wish – not a goal.

A real goal has the following characteristics:
Specific
Measurable
Achievable
Realistic
Time Frame

So, a real goal is S.M.A.R.T. (Specific, Measurable, Achievable, Realistic, Time Frame) These qualities are important, because the goals you set up give you financial targets to achieve. So, instead of saying, "I want to be rich someday," a goal might be:

"I <u>will</u> save $200 every month this year towards my retirement." Note that this is specific. It is also measurable – you will know every single month whether you met that goal or not. A goal should also be achievable and realistic. It should not be so easy that there is no emotional satisfaction after achieving it. It should also not be so difficult that you are likely to fail. Failure invites discouragement, and I don't want you to be discouraged. Of course, a well thought-out goal should have a time frame. The goal, "I will save $200 every month this year towards my retirement" has a monthly and annual time frame. The time frame should be monthly and annual. This way, you will know every month and every year if you met that goal or not.

Action Item for single persons:

> **If you are single and not planning to be married soon, sit down with a pen and paper, and think through what goals you would like to set this year, in the next five years, and in the next 10 – 30 years. <u>Write them down</u>. You are much more likely to achieve goals that are written. Make sure your goals are specific, measurable, achievable, realistic, and have a time frame.**

One of the outcomes of the financial planning process is to give you peace by knowing you are planning well and being a good steward, regardless of marital status. Another outcome is to strengthen the family unit. From a financial standpoint, study after study has shown that one of the primary factors in long-term financial success is staying married. The book <u>The Millionaire Next Door</u> also points this out.

Divorce is highly destructive financially (as well as psychologically and emotionally.) It costs more for two people to live in two separate places than to share a household and its expenses. A study a few years ago showed that expenses typically do not double when couples marry. Expenses tend to go up by the square root of the number of people living in a household. For instance, if there are two people in a household the square root of two equals 1.44. This means it is about 1.44 times more expensive for two people to share a household than for one person to live there alone. It also means that for a family of four the costs are about twice that of a single person, because the square root of the number four (four persons in the house) is two. It also means that if a family of four separates, it will cost about 50% more to support those members than if they had stayed together.

Action Item for a married couple, or those planning marriage soon:

> **For a couple, sit at opposite ends of a table. Each person should list and prioritize his or her short-term, intermediate**

term and long-term goals separately. It is critical that each person prioritizes and ranks his or her goals in order of importance. Once this is done, compare lists. It is very likely the two lists will not match.

That is OK, and perfectly normal. The goal is for both parties to be involved and for each person to have some goals addressed. For instance, assume the husband's number one goal is to take a vacation because the couple hasn't had a nice vacation in several years. Assume the wife's number one goal is to save for retirement because she does not want to spend her retirement years in poverty. At first glance these goals seem incompatible. One is a short-term goal–the vacation, and the other is a long-term goal. Consider proposing that the couple make each of these their first goal. They can save money together both for a vacation and for retirement. Each will know that the other is contributing and sacrificing in order to reach these goals. The husband in this example can look forward to a nice vacation while his wife will feel more secure about her future. Next, the couple can address each person's number two goal, etc. There may not be enough money for all the goals to be met...and that is O.K.

The central point is for couples to work *together* towards their goals. This builds relationship, which is vital both personally and financially. Once your goals are identified,the next step is to automate savings and bill payments, so that you can meet some or all of the goals.

Action Items for this chapter:
1. **Make a list of financial goals. Make sure each goal is specific, measurable, achievable, realistic, and has a time frame.**
2. **Write down these goals and commit to at least three of them.**

Chapter 3

Be An Automatic Success!

This chapter is a short one, but an important one. When you:
- Pay bills
- Pay credit cards
- Save money

…the way to do it successfully is to make it automatic. Sign up with your electricity supplier, your smart phone provider, etc. to auto-draft payment of your bills, either out of your checking account or have them automatically charged to a credit card. Sign up for your full balance on your credit card to also be auto-drafted out of your checking account each month. Have savings, such as for retirement, health insurance, etc., also automatically taken out of your paycheck each pay period. Finally, save for cars, retirement, etc., by having those savings automatically invested or deposited into a savings account as well.

I used to work for a financial services company on both salary and commission. We earned double the commission if we persuaded clients to <u>automatically</u> draft money into investments, instead of physically writing out a check each month. The reason is that if you have to do something each month, it forces you to choose whether to save each month….and almost everyone will choose NOT to save, as something always comes up, like a flat tire or a broken dish-washer (don't ask!). If your savings are automatic, then you won't even miss the money, because it is effortlessly invested each month. There is no check to write, and no decision to make.

It is the same with bills and credit cards. Having payments automatically drafted before the due dates means that you will not have a late-pay that very likely will adversely affect your credit score. Thus, you build wealth each month, automatically, and become an 'automatic success!'

Action Items for this chapter:
1. **Automatically have money taken out of your paycheck and deposited into your 401(k) or 403(b) retirement plan if you have one.**
2. **Automatically have money taken out of your checking account each month to fund an Individual Retirement Account (I.R.A.).**
3. **Automatically pay bills by having them either set up to be charged to credit card or drafted out of your checking account electronically.**
4. **Automatically have loan payments deducted from your checking account each month.**
5. **Set your credit card monthly balance to be automatically drafted out of your checking account each month.**

PART II: DEBT & CREDIT SCORES

Chapter 4

Let's Talk About Debt

(I Have Some Debt…How Much Is OK, and How Much Is Too Much?)

The first thing I want to point out is there is nothing wrong with a limited, manageable amount of debt. Most people could not afford to buy a home without borrowing money for it, for instance. But many people, including those recently graduated from college, get overextended in dollars owed to others as they go along. So…How do you avoid getting into too much debt?

The first step is to recognize that debt is a dangerous thing in some respects. Here is what debt really is: **It is a <u>required</u> certain payment from <u>uncertain</u>, future income.** This means that when you borrow money, you are promising to pay it back in the future from future earnings. Those future earnings you are counting on are not guaranteed. You could lose your job (voluntarily or involuntarily), have hours or pay reduced, get injured, etc. Even if these unhappy things happen, you still have the pay the money back (or risk losing the item for which the money was borrowed.) If you really absorb this idea, you will be more cautious about borrowing money.

Debt also reduces your future discretionary income – the amount of income you use for variable expenses, such as clothes, entertainment, etc. because debt repayment is mandatory, and reduces the money left over for these other items.

So, how much can you safely borrow? If you do not yet own a home, the maximum monthly debt payments (from all debts) should be:

- 15% of net income.

Note that the 15% figure is a ceiling – a maximum. I really think 10% would be better, as it will leave you less financially and emotionally pressured to make payments on the debt each month.

Here is an example:

Julie has gross pay of $6,500.00 each month. After taxes and other deductions, she takes home net pay of $4,200.00 every month from her job as a credit analyst at her bank. $4,200 x 0.15 = $630.00. The most Julie should ever have to pay on all of her debts combined (excluding a mortgage) is $630.00 per month.

A 10% limit ($420.00 for Julie) would be even better. If Julie has a car loan costing her $390.00 per month and a student loan payment costing her $200.00 per month, she already owes $390 + $200 = $590.00 each month…very close to her maximum debt level of $620.00. Julie should not take on any other debt (other than to buy a house) until these are paid off.

Maximum Amount of Debt for Home Owners:

If you own a home, there are two rules:
1) The mortgage payment itself, including property taxes and property insurance, should be a maximum of 25% of your monthly Gross Income.
2) Your total debt payments from all sources (the house payment, car payment, student loan payment, etc.) should be at or below 33% of your monthly gross income.

Using Julie as an example, she has gross pay of $6,500.00 each month. 33% of her gross pay = $6,500 x 0.33 = $2,145 which is the maximum Julie should spend on all debts each month, including a house. Since Julie already owes $590.00 each month on her car loan and student loan, she can buy a home with a maximum monthly payment (including property taxes and insurance) of $2,145.00–$590.00 = $1,555.00 per month.

Here is a word of caution. Banks may approve you for a larger loan than the figures above, for a house. This does not mean you should borrow more. It only means the bank is willing to lend more, because they will earn more interest. The more you borrow, the more they earn. Many people make the assumption that "The bank is the expert…if they approve me for a certain amount, I should borrow that much." This is false. The bank does not have to struggle each month in your house to pay bills, forgo nights out for dinner, etc., when you are squeezed by a big mortgage payment. That is known as being 'house poor' and is not a happy way to live.

In the next chapter, we will cover some debt avoidance strategies.

Action Item for this chapter:

Add up all of your required debt payments for the month and compare them to the ratios in this chapter:

If you do not currently own a home:
- **Maximum debt payments total = 15% of *take-home* pay**

If you do own a home:
- **Maximum debt payments from all sources should be 33% of *gross* pay.**

Chapter 5

How Do I Avoid Excessive Debt?

"If you lack the means to pay, your very bed will be snatched from under you." Proverbs 22:27 (NIV)

Have you ever seen a commercial from a mattress store offering financing to pay for a mattress? I always think of this Proverb when I see one. I want you to have a secure future without being overly burdened by debt. This chapter is about debt <u>avoidance</u>. It is about providing strategies to keep from getting too deeply into debt. Chapter 6 is for those who already find themselves deeply in debt. It is about reducing excess debt.

A few years ago, I was watching a show about my favorite NFL team. The sportscaster said that they could not get good players in the draft, because they were still paying salaries to old players that had retired, and that limited the amount of money they could pay new recruits. When I heard that, I had an epiphany of sorts. I realized the mistake they made was that they had to continue to pay for something that was no longer being used. That led to a whole series of ideas regarding debt. The central point, which I will apply below to credit cards, cars, student loans, and homes, is this:

Make sure the value of item <u>is worth more</u> than the debt used to finance it.

If you will remember this concept, you will be much less likely to have financial distress due to excessive debt in the future.

Let's apply this concept to different areas of debt.

Credit Cards

Avoid charging anything on a credit card that cannot be paid IN FULL each month. When we pay for a meal or gasoline with a credit card, for example, those items are used up almost immediately. Clothes also lose value immediately. A new shirt might cost $50, but once bought and worn, that shirt would only sell for $5.00 or so at a garage sale. Since the value of the item is essentially down to almost zero, you must pay for it immediately, so that the debt does not outlast the value of the shirt. Since you do not want the amount of debt to exceed the value of the item, credit cards must be paid in full each month. This cardinal rule will help you avoid much heartache and financial hassle.

Here is some other interesting information regarding credit cards. I'm sure you have noticed when you shop at Walmart, or Target, or Macy's or Amazon. com, many times you are offered a store-branded credit card, usually with a one-time bonus to entice you to get the card. Merchants, both online and in brick and mortar stores, want you to get their credit card, because:

> People with store branded credit cards tend to shop there twice as much as people who do not have the card. This makes sense, because as a cardholder, you will receive 'special' offers online, in text messages, email, and in the mail to entice you to shop there. Also, you will see the card in your billfold and it will remind you to shop there. This is dangerous, because people then are tempted to spend more than they planned.

Also, people with store branded cards spend on average, twice as much per visit, as those without the card. So, now you can see why merchants try so hard to get you to sign up for their cards. Customers will both visit twice as often online or in a store, and will spend twice as much per visit. This is a recipe for debt disaster.

So, to avoid excessive debt, apply for only <u>one</u> credit card, a MasterCard or Visa Card, and only use it to pay for gasoline. Pay that balance off in full each month. This will prevent you from getting into debt inadvertently.

The reason this is so important is that the average American family carries a credit card balance of over $10,000.00. They did not get there by charging $10,000 all at once. They got there by charging $50 for clothes, $30 for eating out, etc. and not paying off the balance in full each month. Here is an example of the problems that can cause:

If a minimum payment of $200 is made on that $10,000, at 19% interest, it could take almost <u>20 years</u> to pay off the debt, and will cost almost $20,000 in interest, plus the original cost of $10,000.

Think about that…$10,000 worth of purchases costs almost three times as much with interest. How would you feel if you went to the grocery store, and the clerk rang up your groceries, and said "Your total is $150.00. But with our interest charge, you now owe us $450.00 for the groceries!" Yikes! Do not ever put yourself in this position. Never charge more than you can easily pay in full each month.

Having said that, I do encourage you to get at least one credit card in your name. It may surprise some of you that I would suggest that in a financial planning book. But the goal is for you to build a good credit history, so that you can easily buy a home, future cars, etc., later at low interest rates. You must have a good credit history to get low interest rates on future loans. No credit history represents risk to the bank and will result in high interest rates on future loans, because they do not know what you will do. This is the reason I suggest applying for only one MasterCard or Visa card, and charge only gasoline on it. This strategy has the following advantages:
1. You will not get into too much debt on a credit card, since the only purchase is gasoline.
2. The amount charged each month will be relatively stable for most people, since most people drive a similar number of miles most months.
3. You will not use up much available credit on the card.
4. You will build a stronger credit history, and potentially raise your credit score, by paying off this card in full each month.
5. It will be easier to pay off the card each month, since the balance should be in the hundreds, not thousands, of dollars.

Vehicles

Most people borrow money for cars and trucks for five to eight years. The problem is that cars and trucks tend to lose about half of their value every three to five years. For instance, the average new car costs about $30,000. That car will be worth only $15,000 or so in four years. Four years later, it will lose half its value again, and be worth only about $7,500 ($15,000 / 2). And after 12 years that car will only be worth $3000-$4,000 ($7,500 / 2). That loss of value is called depreciation. Cars and trucks depreciate, and relatively quickly.

Remember, the central point regarding debt: **Make sure the value of item is worth more than the debt used to finance it.**

In this case, consider the following example of an eight year loan for a car or truck:

> Assume you are buying a $30,000 vehicle. The loan is at 7% interest. In four years, that vehicle may be worth only $15,000. But you will still owe over $17,000 on it. **This violates the rule that the value of the item should be worth more than the amount owed on it.** The vehicle is only worth $15,000 but you would owe more than $17,000 on it. The loan amount is greater than the value of the item, which harms you financially. This is called being 'upside down' on a loan. Even scarier, car dealers run advertisements encouraging people who are upside down on loans to trade their vehicles in, and the dealer offers to roll the excessive debt into the new loan. So now, that person would start off owing more than the vehicle was worth right off the lot, and making their debt problems even worse. Obviously, you should never do this.

> Let's go back to that original eight year loan for the $30,000 car at 7% interest. After only four years, you would have spent over $6,700 in interest in this example. This means, after only four years of the eight year loan, you will have paid over $19,000 towards both the vehicle and interest, and still owe $17,000. After eight years, you will have paid almost $40,000 for that '$30,000' vehicle, because the interest would be almost $10,000 on the loan. Worse yet, that vehicle is now worth only about $7,500. So, how can you avoid this?

My suggestion is to limit any loan on a vehicle to four years or less. Be aware that car salespersons will try to persuade you to buy a more expensive vehicle, by lengthening the loan, to make it 'appear' to be more affordable. They will say things like, "We can keep your monthly payment at $400 a month. All you have to do is take out a loan that is a little longer." **Remember that financial success is as much about discipline as it is about money.** Stick with the four year loan. This way, the asset (car, truck, SUV) will likely be worth more than the debt throughout the loan, and will outlast the debt. You will have a car or truck that will likely last a decade or longer, and it will be a paid off vehicle in only four years.

Here is a link to an online calculator when considering purchasing a vehicle: http://www.dynamicontent.net/dcv2/indiv_calc.php?calc=21&key=wolfecpa2

A House

At some point, most people want to buy a house. Here is my guidance regarding that purchase. First, you should plan to stay in it for at least five years. There are significant costs associated with buying and selling a home. Those costs can easily top $10,000–$20,000 with commissions, appraisals, inspections, closing costs, title searches, etc. To recoup those costs, you need to stay in a home long enough to give it the opportunity to appreciate (grow in value). Of course, there is no guarantee a home will go up in value, as any investment can rise or fall over time. Even in a rising market, it will typically take time for the house to grow in value enough to offset the costs of buying or selling it.

Once you think you will be located in a place for five years or more, you can consider borrowing money for a home. For this one asset, it is OK to borrow for 15 or 30 years (15 is better) since the asset will still be around and have value after the debt is paid off. Also, generally, homes tend to appreciate, or at least hold their value over time. If you can afford to take out a 15-year loan, it will save significant amounts of interest. For instance, on a $200,000 house at an interest rate of 4.0%, the payment will go up by about $525 per month on a 15 year loan compared to the 30 year loan, but the interest saved will be almost $80,000 compared to the 30-year loan...and you will own the house outright in just 15 years! The other alternative is to go ahead and take out the 30-year loan, and add $525 to the payment each month.

> The interest rate on a 30-year loan will typically be about 0.5% higher on the loan compared to the 15-year loan. However, this will allow some extra financial flexibility if you cannot make the extra payment one month due to unexpected expenses... something the 15-year mortgage does not allow, as the higher payment is locked-in to this loan, since it is shorter.

Here is a link to an online calculator showing interest and principal payments on a 30-year mortgage:
http://www.dynamicontent.net/dcv2/indiv_calc.php?calc=1&key=wolfecpa2
If you are considering a 15-year loan, here is another useful calculator link:

http://www.dynamicontent.net/dcv2/indiv_calc.php?calc=6&key=wolfecpa2

Education

It is OK to borrow for educational expenses, since generally, the earnings benefits will last a lifetime, and income is highly correlated with the amount of education a person receives.

(The more education you have, the more you hopefully will earn.) Remember the rule: **The value of the item should be worth more than the amount owed on it.** Increased income is inherently valuable. The additional earnings from a degree should easily outweigh the debt used to gain the skills that produce the income via education. However, there is a significant caveat to this rule. You should balance the cost of the education against the increased income from the degree, whether undergraduate or graduate degree. For instance, if a Master's degree in education adds $5,000 *per year* in income in a field, and the total cost is $8,000 to get the Master's degree, it seems worthwhile. It would take less than two years to earn back the money spent on the degree. (This is a simplistic example as it does not factor in the taxes on income, but the point is the same.) If a degree in Music costs $50,000 at Juliard, and the increase in income is only $3,000 per year, then that might not be worthwhile. You should seriously look at the increased future income vs. education cost, including lost earnings if you are a full-time student, when making this decision.

Action Items for this chapter:
1. **Pay credit cards in full every month.**
2. **Consider only charging gasoline on a credit card, to minimize credit card debt.**
3. **Limit loans on vehicles to four years or less.**
4. **Add money each month to mortgage payments on a home to shorten the time it takes to pay off a home loan.**
5. **Before getting a graduate degree, compare the costs of the degree to the future income you are likely to receive as a result of the degree.**

Chapter 6

How Do I Get Out of Debt?

"I owe, I owe…it's off to work I go."

Some readers of this book may have accumulated debt before reading this, and may need ideas to help dig out from too much debt. The prior chapter was about avoiding that circumstance…this chapter is about getting rid of debt that is burdensome. You will know if you have too much debt if you follow the guidelines in Chapter 5:

If you do not currently own a home:

Maximum debt payments should be no more than 15% of take-home pay.

If you do own a home:

Maximum debt payments from **all** sources should be no more than 33% of gross pay.

If you find yourself with more debt than that, or if you just feel burdened by the amount of debt you have, implement the following **Action Items:**

1) Stop adding to any existing debt. The analogy is that if there is a flood in a house from a bathtub that has been left on, it does no good to "bail water" unless you first shut off the bathtub. Similarly, the first step to paying down debt is to stop adding to it.

- Stop all charges on credit cards.

- Pay only with checks or cash. Do not use debit cards. People tend to overspend, just as with credit cards, when using debit cards.

2) Consider transferring balances from high interest rate credit cards to low interest rate cards. How do you do this?

Go to www.Bankrate.com, and under 'credit cards' click on 'balance transfer' cards. Read about different offers for low interest rate cards. Choose the card that offers the lowest interest rate on balance transfers for the longest period of time. Then contact them and see if you qualify. If you do qualify, that credit card company will help you transfer balances from a high interest rate credit card to their card. One critical thing – do NOT charge anything on the card to which you are transferring the balance. Use that card only to pay down debt. The goal here is to reduce your debt load. If you charge even one item on this card, that item may be the last thing to which a payment applies, and interest will accrue on charged items. It is a financial trap many people do not realize exists. Again, only use this card to pay down balances transferred to it. Never charge an item on this card. When you get towards the end of a low interest rate promotion and your credit card debt is not paid off, go back to Bankrate.com and apply for a different balance transfer card, and continue the process.

3) **Always pay more than the 'minimum payment' on a credit card,** whether it in an existing card with a balance or a 'balance transfer card'. The minimum payment is typically only about 2% of the balance. It will take many years to pay off accumulated debt if you only pay the minimum. Here is some financial motivation to pay more than the minimum due on a credit card:

On a typical $10,000 average balance on a credit card, the minimum payment is around $200 per month (2% of $10,000). Adding just $100 per month can cut the repayment period IN HALF! And the interest cost could drop from $20,000 to $8,000; a savings of $12,000...depending on the interest rate on the card! Of course, $8,000 interest on a $10,000 credit card debt is still a lot of interest. So, by both paying off as much as possible each pay period, and utilizing lower interest rate cards, you can save potentially thousands of dollars in interest.

4) Consider using youneedabudget.com to allocate how much money goes to prior debts each pay period. Pay down as much debt as possible each pay period, by minimizing other expenses. Again, **financial success is as much about discipline as it is about money.**

5) Consider consolidating debts with a loan from a bank if the interest rate is lower. However, I advise that you avoid home equity loans to pay off credit cards. While most recent college graduates may not own a home, some may. If you own a home, home equity loans allow you to take out an additional loan against your home, and borrow against the equity you have built up over time. However, this equity is an asset, and equity in a house is, in a way, forced savings. Savings are easy to spend, and hard to accumulate. So, do not borrow against your house to repay other debts.

6) If the amount owed is genuinely excessive and overwhelming, consider the Consumer Credit Counseling Service (credit.org). This service offers free counseling. They also offer a debt management plan, but this plan has strict requirements. It requires clients to close all credit card accounts and to suspend any applications for other loans until the debts are paid off. The debt management plan will try to negotiate lower interest rates on credit cards on your behalf. There is a cost to you for this debt management plan, if you choose to implement it.

7) Avoid declaring bankruptcy, if possible. Bankruptcy will stay on your credit report for ten years. Financial institutions will be unlikely to lend to you for cars, a home, or any other reason. Those that do will allow the loan only at the highest rates.

Action Items for this chapter:
1. **If you feel overwhelmed by debt, stop all charges on credit cards immediately.**
2. **Consider transferring balances on credit cards to other credit card companies if they offer lower interest rates.**
3. **Always pay more than the minimum due on credit cards if you have credit card debt that is not paid off.**

Chapter 7

Go For The High Score! (Credit Scores)

Parent to child: "Did you make a high score?"

In this chapter, you will find information regarding your credit score, what it is, and why it is important to make a high score, just like in school!

Everyone in the United States who has borrowed money has a credit score. The scary thing is that many college students and recent graduates do not have a score, because they have not taken out any credit. Of course, some college graduates do have a credit score, due to student loan debt or credit cards, but they do not know what the score is, or why it matters.

This score is important because the higher your credit score, the better a credit risk you are perceived to be by lenders. That means you are likely to qualify for lower interest rates on everything from cars to homes to credit cards to student loans. Those lower interest rates mean *you can save potentially hundreds of thousands of dollars* over a lifetime in interest. Conversely, lower credit scores send the signal that you are a higher credit risk, and thus will be charged higher rates of interest when you need to borrow money.

Employers also look at credit scores because studies have shown that employees who have low scores tend to be less productive at work. So, keeping your score high is important for job security as well, even if you have no immediate plans to borrow money.

There are many companies that measure credit risk using credit scores, but the most widely used one is Fair Isaac Corporation, or FICO. They look at different items and come up with a credit score. (Not surprisingly, their score is called a 'FICO Score'!) That score can be as low as 300 (Terrible) or as high as 850 (Perfect). People with scores above 750 usually qualify for the lowest interest rates available. For instance, Honda might run a commercial for an Accord sedan, offering rates as low as 0.9% for three years, for their highest qualifying customers. That's what they mean when they say, "With Approved Credit" in the commercials or pop-up ads. That advertised low interest rate will typically only be offered to those with high FICO scores.

So, what goes into a credit score by FICO? There are five pieces: Credit History, Amount Owed, Length of Credit, New Credit, and Type of Credit.

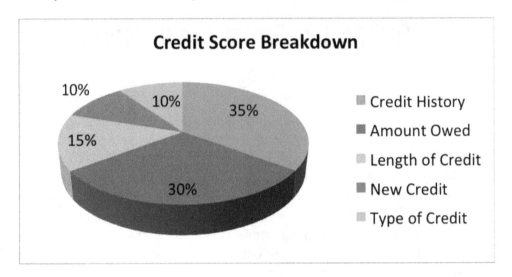

Credit Score Breakdown

- Credit History
- Amount Owed
- Length of Credit
- New Credit
- Type of Credit

Credit History is the single most important piece, and it counts 35% towards your total score. This is your personal record of paying on time or paying late, and paying the amount owed. All kinds of information go into this. Electric bill payments, smart phone payments, rent or mortgage payments, credit card bill payments, even library fines, etc. all factor into credit history. It is critical to pay all of your bills, on time, in the amount owed, every single month, without exception. Just one late payment on a bill could drop your FICO score by as much as 100 points. A drop from a high score of 760 to a mediocre score of 660, for instance, could add tens of thousands of dollars to the cost of a home in a 30-year fixed mortgage, due to the higher interest rate charged. If you have paid bills late up to now, start paying on time as of this month. Over the next year or two, your score will rise as your history of paying bills on time improves.

The Amount Owed is the second largest piece in the Credit Score pie chart, counting 30% towards your overall score. This is the amount owed on credit cards, student loans, mortgages, car loans, etc. FICO looks at both the total amount of required payments relative to your income, and the amount owed to each creditor. One way to aim for a higher credit score is to avoid charging too much on any single credit card. Credit card companies give you an 'available credit' when you open an account. It is important to keep the amount owed on a card at a maximum of 30% of available credit.

Here is an example: Matt has a Chase Ink credit card, and Chase gives Matt $5,000 available credit on his new card. This means that Matt could charge as much as $5,000 on that card. However, it would be wise for Matt to keep the amount owed on his Chase Ink card at $1,500 or less. ($5,000 x 30% = $1,500.00) The reason is that FICO interprets higher balances relative to available credit as a sign of poor credit management on the part of the card holder. So, if Matt's balance on the card rose to $3,000, then $4,000, then $5,000, his credit score would go down. The more you owe on a card compared to its available credit, the lower your credit score is likely to be, once you pass that 30% threshold.

The Amount Owed in the pie chart above also evaluates your total debt from all lenders. It is important to limit non-mortgage debt to 15% of your net pay, if possible. If you owe more as you read this book, then pay down existing debt until you are under this threshold.

Length of Credit is the third largest component in a FICO score. It counts 15% towards the overall score. The longer you have accounts open, the more stable you appear to be to lenders and to Fair Isaac, and the higher your credit score will be. Some people open and close credit card accounts often. Do not do that! It will adversely impact your credit score. If you want a credit card, open one account–two at most–and use them for years, paying them on time and in full each month, of course.

New Credit counts 10% towards your score. If you only open a credit card account every few years, or take on a car loan, these will appear as 'New Credit' and will potentially raise your score. However, if you open multiple accounts, such as credit card accounts, in a short period of time (a few months) this will cause your score to go down. It sends the message (accurately or not) that either you are desperate for credit or that you are less stable financially.

Finally, Types of Credit count 10% towards your credit score. If you have different types of credit, and manage them well, such as a car loan and credit card, your score will rise modestly. It sends the message that you can handle diverse payments well. I do not think you need to take on additional debt just to add a new type of credit, to raise your score, however. This is just 10% of the score.

So, how do you check your score?

Action Item: Go to <u>annualcreditreport.com</u>. At that site, federal law allows you go obtain one credit report each year from each of three major credit reporting agencies for free! (Hey, that's a good use of money!)

There are three major credit bureaus that track your credit:
- Equifax,
- Experian and,
- TransUnion.

You should check all three at least once a year, and **get your credit score with the report.** You may have to pay a nominal amount for the credit score. Another strategy is to get one report, every four months – one from each of the three credit reporting agencies (thus rotating them every four months through the year). Contact information for each of these is below, and in the Appendix.

When you get your report, read through it carefully. Make sure any loan balances and history of repayment are correct, and that all the information, including your name, addresses (current and past), etc. are all correct. **It is estimated that one in four files has inaccurate credit information.** Inaccurate information can lead to lower credit scores. Contact the agency at the web sites below to report any problem with your credit report:

Equifax: www.equifax.com
Experian: www.experian.com
Transunion: transunion.com/disputeonline

Note that credit scores vary from firm to firm somewhat, and that FICO has different versions of scores. However, if the information is accurate in your reports, the scores should not be far apart. If they are, that is a red flag that something may be wrong with a credit report.

Action Items for this chapter:
1) **Get a credit report from <u>annualcreditreport.com</u> once a year.**
2) **Check your credit reports at least once a year from Equifax, Experian and TransUnion.**
3) **Check your credit score from Equifax, Experian and TransUnion once a year, or before you plan to take out a loan.**
4) **Always pay your bills on time.**
5) **Limit charges to 30% of the available credit on any credit card.**
6) **Avoid applying for multiple credit cards in a short period of time.**

Chapter 8

Credit Cards - Things to Know

In the previous chapter, I suggested that you get a credit card so that you can build a good credit history. However, the goal of this book is for you to do well financially, and not to be burdened by debt. So, here are some things to know about credit cards:

1. You should pay the total bill that is due every month before the due date. If the card is paid in full each month, there will not be any interest charges on the card. That is a very good thing.

2. Set up 'automatic payments' and choose to 'pay the balance billed in full' with the credit card company, as opposed to writing them a check each month. This way, the payment will not be late or lost due to the postal service.

3. Do not get a 'cash advance' or 'cash back' using a credit card. Most credit cards charge a 3% fee immediately for this, and also start charging interest <u>immediately</u>, many times at a very high 15%–29% rate of interest on the cash. Many cards charge interest on the purchases as well as the cash if this is done. If you must do this, be sure to pay all of this off as soon as the bill comes. A credit card is not a debit card, even though they look similar. Only use your debit card for cash withdrawals or 'cash back' such as at the grocery store.

4. Cover the numbers of the credit card with your hand when in public. Many people looking over your shoulder can get your number when it is out of your wallet or purse.

5. If you are finding yourself needing to charge more than 30% of the available credit each month, call the credit card company and request a 'credit line increase.' If you have paid the card in full each month for at least six months to a year, the company is much more likely to raise the credit line. (Remember, your credit score goes down as your charges exceed 30% of the available credit...thus the need to keep charges below this threshold.)

6. Read your credit card contract. After reading it, call the credit card company with any questions you have. It is important to understand the contracts to which you have agreed.

7. Know the benefits of your credit card. Some credit cards offer perks such as airline miles, hotel points, lost baggage allowance, extended warranties, etc. I always take a copy of these perks when I travel, so that if I need them, I will know how they work when I call the credit card company.

8. Always check your credit card statement each month to make sure the charges are correct. Also make sure that there are no fraudulent charges or mistakes. When I was in graduate school, I bought a lawn mower. But the credit card statement showed two charges...for two mowers! I called the credit card company and they investigated, and erased the error for the extra mower.

9. If you suspect fraud (such as a charge you did not make), contact the credit card company as soon as you find the charge. If they determine that your credit card number may have been compromised, they will suspend the charge and send you out a new card. You are not responsible for fraudulent charges, as long as you notify the company within 48 hours (in most cases) of notification of those charges.

10. Many credit cards will allow you to suspend a charge if the good or service you receive is defective, and the merchant will not replace the item or refund the money. If this happens, contact the credit card company and challenge the charge. To be effective, most challenges of this type must be in writing rather than just a phone call. Note that you must first provide evidence that you contacted the merchant first and that they failed to resolve the situation to your satisfaction. Certainly, the merchant may require the defective product be returned prior to refunding any money. They may also require you to pay for return shipping, depending on the merchant.

Action Items for this chapter:

1. Pay credit cards in full every month.
2. Avoid 'cash advances' from credit cards.
3. Limit charges on credit cards to 30% or less of the available credit on the card.
4. Review your credit card statement each month. Make sure the charges are correct and that there are no errors.
5. If you find an error, contact the credit card company and challenge the charge.

PART III: EMPLOYEE BENEFITS & INSURANCE

Chapter 9

Get All The Benefits You Deserve

OK...I have to confess. One of my goals in writing this book has been to keep the chapters short. This one is longer. Forgive me for that, but please don't stop reading just because this chapter is a little longer! Here's the reason you need to know the information in this chapter: **Employee benefits on average are worth the equivalent of two month's salary. That's over 15% of your total pay. At 40 hours a week, your benefits are worth over 300 hours of work.** Yet, almost no one knows any details about their employee benefits. If they are this valuable, you need to know about them! So, I am covering them here.

When you go to work for an employer, you will commonly be offered a package of benefits, which may include some or all of the following:
- Health insurance
- Cancer insurance
- Flexible Savings Account (FSA) for Child Care
- Flexible Savings Account (FSA) for Healthcare
- Health Savings Account (HSA)
- Life insurance
- Disability insurance
- Dental insurance
- 401(k) or 403(b) retirement plans
- Pension

Each year, you will typically re-enroll in your employer's benefits plan. This book is meant to provide sound basic information for financial decisions, and these topics can be very complex. So, my goal is to provide enough basic information so that you understand your benefits and can make good decisions regarding them.

The first thing you should realize is that the vast majority of people have no idea how their benefits package works. They don't know their costs, limitations, or what they provide. So, the first Action Item is this:

Action Item: Get the information regarding each of your benefits at work (Human Resources has this information) and take time to read about each area of benefits.

Next, I will cover different areas of employee benefits that are commonly offered.

Health Insurance

One of the scariest things I know from personal experience as a professor is that many people in their 20's go without health insurance. Studies also bear this out. This is true even though the Affordable Care Act (Obamacare) requires people to have health insurance, or be subject to an increasing fine. If you are not covered by health insurance as you read this, get covered immediately. Adults under the age of 26 can be covered on their parent's plan. You also may be able to get coverage on your own, or get coverage through your employer or through your spouse's employer if you are married.

Most people in their 20's assume that they will be healthy, and that they do not need health insurance. This is poor planning for the following reasons.

First, you might be in a car wreck. One or two nights in intensive care can easily top $100,000. Can you pay that? The hospital will sue you and garnish your future wages...for years if necessary–if you cannot and are uninsured. Many people mistakenly think hospitals will just let bills go unpaid. However, hospitals are known to be some of the most aggressive debt collectors around. They have to, to remain open.

Second, you never know when a health event will occur. I had kidney stones when I was in law school. They were completely unexpected. Had I not had health insurance, the out of pocket costs for my hospitalization in today's dollars would have topped $50,000. That was just three days in the hospital.

I also have had students that were diagnosed with cancer, and did not have insurance. Many students just think, "It won't happen to me...I'm healthy." But think about it. Almost all medical issues are initially surprises – and unexpected, including cancer, heart problems, kidney stones, and on and on. Many people mistakenly think they can just save money by paying the tax penalty in Obamacare rather than get covered by health insurance. If a health event happens, whether due to a body issue or automobile wreck, the financial consequences are potentially catastrophic...for a lifetime. The issue is not whether you can afford health insurance. **The fact is you cannot afford to be without it.** If health insurance is not offered by your employer, consider using www. ehealthinsurance.com to find an affordable plan.

So, the next Action Item is this:

> **Action Item: If you or a family member are not covered by health insurance, get covered immediately.**

Next, I will explain the basics of how most health insurance policies work. There are usually three separate costs:

1) The Premium: This is the amount you pay to the insurance company for the health insurance. It is paid regardless of how much health insurance you use.

2) The Deductible: A deductible is the amount a covered individual must pay out-of-pocket for covered health costs before insurance coverage begins paying for expenses. This is a completely separate cost from the premiums. For instance, a health plan might have a $2,000 deductible. This means that you would have to have $2,000 in covered medical costs before the insurance would start paying any covered bills related to healthcare.

   Deductibles are usually annual deductibles in policies. The year the policy runs might be a calendar year, or a fiscal year. For instance, a health plan might run from Sept. 1st each year to Aug 31st the following year. This means the deductible would apply each year. If you had paid $2,000 in covered health costs by February, for instance, the insurance company would start paying some costs from that point to the end of August in the example above. On September 1st, the deductible would start over each year.

   In most health insurance plans there is an individual deductible as well as a maximum family deductible. A common individual deductible might be $2,000 and a common maximum family deductible might be $6,000 per calendar year. Once the annual deductible is met, medical costs are shared with the insurance carrier. This is the third type of medical cost:

3) Co-Insurance. Co-insurance applies when costs are shared with the insurance company. Commonly, the individual or family might pay 20% of this portion while the insurer would pay the remaining 80% of costs, up to a cap, such as $5,000 for an individual, or $10,000 for a family. If and when medical expenses exceed the co-insurance cap during the calendar or fiscal year, most insurance plans typically pay 100% of costs above this amount.

For example, assume John has $20,000 in medical costs. He has a health insurance plan with a $2,000 annual deductible, then co-insurance that pays 80% of the next $5,000 in costs. John is responsible for the remaining 20% of the $5,000 in costs after the deductible. Note…that $5,000 limit for co-insurance is in <u>addition to</u> the deductible.

Here is an example of the how a policy like this might work:

$20,000   Total medical costs

      minus $2,000   Deductible paid by John

      minus $1,000   Co-Insurance (20% of next $5,000 in covered costs)

             $3,000   Total Out-of-Pocket Costs Paid by John

$17,000   Amount of covered medical costs covered by health insurance

When evaluating health insurance plans, it is important to know what the co-insurance rate and monetary amount to which it applies will be before selecting a plan. Note that deductibles do not include the premiums paid for health insurance. Only actual out-of-pocket medical costs apply to the deductible or co-insurance owed by the covered party.

Cancer Insurance

If you are offered a cancer insurance policy, strongly consider rejecting it. The purpose of health insurance is to protect against a catastrophic loss due to medical costs. Cancer insurance only deals with…cancer. It does not cover heart attacks, kidney stones, automobile accidents, etc. Instead, use the money you would have spent on this limited insurance and use it to get covered by a health insurance plan that covers you for health care costs, regardless of the cause.

Flexible Savings Account (FSA) for Dependent Care (Child Care)

A Flexible Savings Account (FSA) for <u>dependent care</u> is an account that may be offered by your employer to help pay for child care expenses for your children under the age of 13 so that you can work. The big benefit is that you will not owe income taxes on the money you put in the account, as long as it is used for child care. Child care costs include child care payments to centers, but also things like tuition and fees for pre-school and school from Kindergarten through sixth grade if a child is in a private school.

How much could you save in taxes if you deposit money into an FSA for Childcare? Here is an example: Assume Janice saves $2,000 in an FSA and she is in the 25% income tax bracket. She will cut her income tax bill by $500! ($2,000 x 0.25 = $500 tax savings.) If you are single, you can deposit up to $2,550 a year in an FSA Dependent Care account in 2016. That is a total amount…not a per-child amount. That amount will go up over time to adjust for inflation in future years. If you are married, you can deposit up to $5,000 in the account in 2016.

There are a couple of downsides to Dependent Care FSA's, however. First, you must spend the money each calendar year in the account, or you forfeit any remaining balance to your employer. If you have a child under 13 and you are working, estimate how much you spend on childcare or private school costs each year, and put that amount in the Dependent Care FSA if it is offered to you. The second item is that you have keep receipts of child care costs, and submit them to your employer's FSA for reimbursement. Unlike an FSA for Healthcare (see below) you cannot borrow money from this account before you have deposited it, to pay for child care. You have to submit receipts to be reimbursed. You should keep copies of these receipts with your tax records so that you will have proof of the child care expenses. Here is a summary of the Dependent Care FSA:

- The child must be your child or a legally adopted child.

- You must provide more than 50% of the support for the child.
- The child must be under the age of 13 to qualify for this FSA.
- Private school tuition is included in this FSA. You can be reimbursed for these expenses as well.
- Expenses must be paid so that you can work…you cannot use this FSA for a stay-at-home parent.
- Money is taken out of your paycheck into a Dependent Care FSA account each pay period. You can decide how much each year to take out of your paycheck and deposit into the FSA.
- The maximum amount you can deposit in a Dependent Care FSA in 2016 is $2,550 if you are a single parent or $5,000 if you are married. Every dollar deposited in the FSA is income tax free, which saves money on taxes.
- You will file a claim for reimbursement of the dependent care expenses with the FSA. You can do this whenever you would like. You can do this monthly, quarterly, or just once a year. You must claim the reimbursement by year-end or else the money is forfeited.
- You should keep a copy of the receipts for child care and file them with your taxes. In case of an audit, you will have proof that you actually incurred the expenses.

There are other rules for FSA's that are beyond the scope of this book – check with your employer for details. But the key items are listed above.

Flexible Savings Account (FSA) for Healthcare

A Flexible Savings Account (FSA) for <u>healthcare</u> is an account that may be offered by your employer to help pay for out-of-pocket medical expenses, such as health insurance deductibles, co-pays for doctor's visits and prescription costs. The money you save in an FSA for Healthcare also is not taxed, as long as it is spent on health care.

It is a <u>separate</u> account from the FSA for Dependent Care. You can use the money in the FSA Healthcare account to pay for out-of-pocket costs such as payments to the dentist, eye exams, prescription eye glasses, and contacts, or laser eye surgery. (Note: Over-the-counter items like aspirin, contact solution, toothpaste, etc. are <u>not</u> covered.) You can even withdraw money from the FSA for Healthcare before it has been deposited (i.e. essentially borrow from the account). For instance, if you are planning on a $2,000 medical expense, such as LASIK on your eyes, you could withdraw the $2,000 from your Healthcare

FSA in January or February and have the procedure. Your contributions the rest of the year would repay the account. Note that this only applies to FSA's for Healthcare. You cannot borrow money ahead of time in a Dependent Care FSA.

You cannot use money in an FSA to pay for health insurance premiums, or non-prescription costs or over the counter medicines, such as toothpaste or ibuprofen. The maximum amount that you can contribute is $2,550 in an FSA Healthcare account in 2016. The amount you can contribute in future years will go up with inflation over time. (You can type 'FSA Healthcare Contribution Limit' into a search engine in the future.) If you open an FSA and put money into it, that money is not taxed for income tax purposes. So, for instance, if you save $2,550 in an FSA and you are in the 25% income tax bracket, that will save you $637.50 ($2,550 x 0.25 = $637.50) in income taxes.

There is a downside to FSA's however. You must spend the money each calendar year in the account, or you forfeit any remaining balance to your employer. There is a $500 exception – up to $500 can be rolled over to the first few months of the following year, but only if the plan by your employer allows it. Amounts remaining at the end of the year that exceed that are forfeited to your employer. Read your employer plan carefully to see if the $500 exception is allowed.

To estimate how much you should deposit in a Healthcare FSA, track what you spend on doctor's visits and prescriptions each year, and put that amount in the FSA if it is offered to you. Here is a summary of the Health Care FSA:

- Money is taken out of your paycheck into a Healthcare FSA account each pay period. This account is separate from the Dependent Care FSA, if you have that as well. You can decide how much each year to take out of your paycheck and deposit into the FSA.
- The most you can deposit in a Healthcare FSA in 2016 is: $2,550 (Single) or $5,000 (Married).
- Every dollar deposited in the FSA is income tax free, which saves money on taxes.
- You will file a claim for reimbursement of the health care expenses with the FSA. You can do this whenever you would like. You can do this monthly, quarterly, or just once a year. You must claim the reimbursement by year-end or else the money is forfeited. There is a $500 exception that some employers may offer.
- Unlike a Dependent Care FSA, you can 'withdraw' money from a Healthcare FSA before it is credited to the account. I.E. You can borrow money interest free to pay for a health expense and pay it back through the rest of the year.

- You should keep a copy of the receipts for health care and file them with your taxes. In case of an audit, you will have proof that you actually incurred the expenses.

There is an even better account option which is available through some employers, below.

Health Savings Account

A Health Savings Account (HSA) is an account that may be offered by your employer to help pay for out-of-pocket medical expenses, such as health insurance deductibles, co-pays for doctor's visits and prescription costs. You can also use the money to pay for out-of-pocket costs to the dentist, eye exams, prescription eye glasses, and contacts. (Over the counter products, such as contact solution, etc. are not covered.) You can open an HSA if you are covered by a 'high deductible health plan' by your employer. You need to check with your employer to see if your health insurance is a 'high deductible' plan. If it is, and your employer offers you the option of opening an HSA, strongly consider saving money in it. HSA's are similar to FSA's in the following ways:
- You can use the money to pay for out-of-pocket medical expenses, like glasses, co-pays at doctor's offices.
- The money you save in the account is income tax free, as long as you use it for qualified health expenses.
- You cannot use money in it to pay for health insurance premiums, or non-prescription costs or over the counter medicines, such as toothpaste or ibuprofen.

However, HSA's have some significant <u>advantages</u> over FSA's for healthcare:
- You can save more in an HSA:
  - o $3,350 (Single)
  - o $6,750 (Family)
  - o These are the total amounts that you and your employer can deposit in an HSA in 2016. These contribution limits are indexed for inflation and will gradually rise in future years. *Check with your employer to find the limits in future years.*
- **There is no requirement that you spend all the money each year. If you have money left over, it can roll over to the next year. That is not true in Flexible Spending Accounts.**

- Earnings in the account can also grow income tax <u>free</u>, as long as they are spent on qualifying medical expenses.
- **This account can keep growing until retirement.**
- **When retired, this health savings account could be used to pay for medical expenses, <u>tax free</u>, during those years, when medical costs are likely to be higher.**
- You need to keep receipts showing money spent from an HSA was spent on a qualifying medical expense. Otherwise, the IRS may impose income taxes, and a 20% penalty on the amounts withdrawn. Keep those receipts in your tax records.

There is one significant disadvantage of using an HSA compared to a Flexible Spending Account:
- Unlike a Health Care FSA, you <u>cannot</u> 'borrow' money from a Health Care FSA before it is credited to the account for a large medical expense. I.E. You cannot borrow money that is not in the account.

Here is a summary of the Health Savings Account (HSA):
- Money is taken out of your paycheck into the HSA account each pay period. This account is separate from any FSA, if you have one.
- You can decide how much each year to take out of your paycheck and deposit into the HSA.
- The most you and your employer can deposit in a HSA in 2016 is: $3,350 if you are single. If you are married, you can deposit up to $6,750 in 2016.
- If you open a HSA only for yourself, you can only be reimbursed for your own medical expenses. If you are married, and fund a family HSA, it can be used to reimburse medical expenses for anyone in your nuclear family (you, your spouse and children.)
- Every dollar deposited in the HSA is income tax free, which saves money on taxes.
- You can either use an HSA debit card associated with the account to pay for health care expenses, or you can file a claim for reimbursement of the health care expenses from the HSA.
- You should keep a copy of the receipts for health care and file them with your taxes. In case of an audit, you will have proof that you actually incurred the expenses.

Since money in an HSA is not subject to income taxes, and you can keep this money growing until retirement to pay for health care costs, consider opening an HSA if you qualify and if it is offered.

Life Insurance

Many employers provide life insurance as an employee benefit. In some plans, the employer may just pay for the life insurance. In other plans, the employer may pay for some life insurance, and allow you to purchase additional life insurance without evidence of insurability (i.e. without additional health questions, blood tests, etc.) It is usually preferable to buy as much life insurance as your employer will allow you to purchase. However, if you do not sign up when first hired, some group plans do not allow you to buy life insurance later. So...it is a good idea to purchase it when it is first offered.

Single people without anyone depending on them for support (such as a child or spouse) do not really need a lot of life insurance. However, I encourage you to sign up for life insurance with your employer even if you are single so that you will have some locked in. That way, if a health event occurs later which makes it difficult to qualify for life insurance you will still have some.

Once you are married or have a child, however, each spouse will need a lot of life insurance...typically between 12 – 15 times each spouse's gross wages. For instance, if you earn $60,000 in your job, you need a total of between $720,000 and $900,000 of life insurance if you have any children or a spouse. Employers will not usually offer that much, but may offer some. Employers who offer life insurance typically offer 1-4 times your gross salary in life insurance. So, it is a good start. You can consider buying additional life insurance through a life insurance company. I discuss that in a separate chapter of this book.

Beneficiaries in a Life Insurance Policy

Beneficiaries are the persons to whom your life insurance proceeds go to, in the event of your death. (I know this is not fun to think about, but the purpose of this book is to give you good basic financial information.) When you sign up for a life insurance policy, including one with your employer, you should list at least one primary beneficiary and one contingent beneficiary.

A primary beneficiary is someone who will receive the life insurance proceeds if you die while covered. If you have more than one primary beneficiary, you will need to list the percentage you would like each to receive. For instance, if you have two siblings who you would like to be primary beneficiaries, you need to list them both with the percentage you would like each to receive. The percentages must add up to 100%. **Be sure to list primary beneficiaries by specific name, their Social Security number, and relation.** For example: 'my sister, Jennifer Gomez, Social Security number 555-66-5757'. Do NOT leave the beneficiary section blank, and do not list your estate as the beneficiary. If you do not fill out the beneficiary section, the life insurance will go to your estate, which must go through probate. Probate will add complication and costs, and delay payment of the life insurance to your survivors.

A <u>contingent</u> beneficiary is someone who will receive the life insurance proceeds if you die while covered, and the primary beneficiary is not alive at that time. For instance, you might list your husband, Bill Montgomery, as the primary beneficiary. You might list your parents, Jeff Davidson and Elizabeth Davidson as contingent beneficiaries. This would mean that if your husband predeceased you, or if you died together, your parents would receive the life insurance proceeds. Just as for primary beneficiaries, if you have more than one contingent beneficiary, you will need to list the percentage you would like each to receive. The percentages must add up to 100%. Be sure to list contingent beneficiaries by specific full name, Social Security number, and relation as well.

Disability Insurance

If your employer offers Disability Insurance coverage, sign up for it. Here is the reason you need it:
- More than 50% of Americans between the ages of 25 and 65 will be disabled for at least a three month period at some point before reaching age 65.
- That is three continuous months…not a few days every once in a while.
- 10% of those disabilities are permanent disabilities.

It may seem as though that possibility is remote, but it is a catastrophic financial loss as well as an emotional hit if it happens. So, sign up for this disability coverage with your employer when it is offered. Read your benefits package so that you know what is covered and how much you might receive if disabled.

Typical employer-provided policies only cover 60% of <u>base</u> pay if you become disabled. Can you afford a 40% pay cut? Most people cannot. This means you will need to buy a supplementary disability policy on your own, to add to any coverage your employer provides.

Also, most employer plans only cover disability for two years. After two years, many employer plans use a definition of disability called 'any occupation.' This means that if you can do anything to earn a living – such as say, "Welcome to Walmart" then you are not disabled under the policy and will receive nothing. 98% of disabilities are disqualified under this 'any occupation' definition. This means that if you end up with a disability lasting longer than two years, your disability benefits will end after two years, and you will be stuck financially with a catastrophic loss of income.

If your employer offers you the choice to pay the premiums after-tax (so that you are taxed on the premiums each pay period) choose this option. It will cost just a little more each pay period, but it will allow disability payments, if the need arises, to be income tax-free to you.

Also, in regards to disability insurance offered by your employer, look carefully at the waiting periods (sometimes called elimination periods) in the plan. The longer the waiting period that you choose, the lower the cost of the disability insurance. The reason is that the waiting period is the time period between the disabling event (such as a car crash) and the time that the employee receives a disability payment. The longer the waiting period, the more likely the person will recover and will not need the insurance – hence the lower cost. For many people, three to six months is an affordable option – but evaluate your own choice carefully.

Many employer-provided disability plans only replace about 60% of base income, and also have restrictive definitions of disability. To make up for that shortfall, I recommend purchasing an individual disability policy to make up the difference from a reputable company, such as USAA or Northwestern Mutual insurance. Make sure the definition of disability is 'own occupation' to age 65. This means you will be considered disabled if you cannot perform the material duties of your own occupation, based on your training, experience and education. Thus, you are more likely to be covered and paid under the policy if a disabling event occurs. You can choose a longer waiting period, such as three to six months, to help lower the premiums.

Dental Insurance

Some employers offer dental insurance as an employee benefit. Generally, I suggest signing up for this coverage, as care for teeth can be expensive. Many people think health insurance covers dental work or cleanings. It does not. Health insurance does not cover dental expenses. Dental work is a separate item. Read your plan to evaluate the costs, benefits, and limitations regarding who can be your dentist in the plan.

Action Items for this chapter:
1) **Get the information for all of your benefits at work and take time to read them and understand them.**
2) **If needed, modify your choices in terms of the benefits offered by your employer.**
3) **If you or a family member are not covered by health insurance, get covered immediately.**
4) **Sign up for health insurance offered by your employer. If it is not offered and you do not have health insurance coverage, sign up for health insurance from a source such as <u>ehealthinsurance.com</u>.**
5) **Sign up for life insurance offered by your employer.**
6) **Sign up for disability insurance offered by your employer.**
7) **Consider adding your own life insurance and disability insurance to supplement any coverage your employer provides.**

Chapter 10

Retirement Plans: 401(k)'s, 403(b)'s and Pensions

As recent college graduates, many of you will be or may already be eligible to save for retirement in a retirement plan offered by your employer. Only about 50% of American workers have such an option…so if you do, take advantage of it! While there are a myriad of plans, the most common ones are 401(k) plans, 403(b) plans, and pension plans.

401(k) and 403(b) retirement plans are similar in most respects, and so I will discuss them together. 401(k) plans are offered by for-profit companies, and 403(b) plans are offered by non-profit entities, such as private hospitals and private universities. They are each named after the tax code provision that created them.

When people talk about 401(k) plans, you often hear about advantages such as:

- Free money from your employer.
- Lower taxable income.
- Savings and earnings that accumulate without your having to remember to make deposits.
- The opportunity to retire and not have to worry about money!

Does this sound too good to be true? It isn't. It is what you can gain from investing in your company's 401(k) or 403(b) plan. 401(k) and 403(b) plans are two of the most popular retirement plans around.

As a recent college graduate, retirement may be the farthest thing from your mind. But think about how much of a difference 10, 20, or 30 or more years can make in terms of compound interest. (I show you how much a difference just a few years can make in the chapter titled, 'You Work For Money – Make Money Work for You!') If your employer offers a 401(k) or 403(b) plan, you should participate in it as soon as possible. If you start early, you very well may have a couple of million dollars (or more) in your account by the time you retire.

How does a 401(k) or 403(b) plan work?
1. When you participate in a 401(k) or 403(b) plan, you tell your employer how much money you want to deduct from your paycheck into the plan.
2. The money you contribute comes out of your check *before* taxes are calculated, and more importantly, before you ever have a chance to spend it. That makes the 401(k) or 403(b) one of the most painless ways to save for retirement. The savings are *automatic* each pay period.
3. In many plans, your employer will match a portion of your contribution. That means if you put money into the plan, your employer may put some in, too. That is free money…don't EVER turn it down! Your employer wants you to participate in the plan because of compliance issues (which we won't worry about in this book). The matched amount they offer (the free money part) is your incentive to participate.
4. The money is invested, at your direction, in mutual funds, bond funds, etc. Your employer does not choose your investments—you do that. Your retirement plan will usually have a list of investments from which you can choose as well as some guidelines for the level of risk you are willing to take. I will address that later.

Again, these plans allow you to save money, pre-tax, out of your paycheck and invest it in the offerings in the plan. This means that you will pay less in taxes than if you did not participate in the plan when you save money in it. You can contribute up to $18,000 per year in 2016 if you are 49 years of age or younger, and up to $24,000 per year if you are 50 or older. These contribution limits will gradually rise in future years.

Many employers offer a <u>matching</u> contribution if you will participate in the plan. What that means is that if you take money out of your gross pay and save it for retirement in a 401(k) or 403(b), the employer will put money in as well. A common match is 3% of income, but some employers match more. In this example, a 3% match would give you a 100% return on the first 3% of your pay that you saved.

You would <u>double</u> your money, just by committing to saving it! Imagine if a bank had a pop-up ad that said, "Deposit money with us, and we'll match it, dollar-for-dollar, plus interest." That is what your employer is offering you with a match. Some plans match 50 cents for every dollar up to 6% or more instead. That is still fantastic – it would be a 50% return instantly. The important thing is to immediately start saving for retirement. Do not turn down saving in these employer-sponsored plans if you are eligible. Be sure to always contribute enough to get the whole match. 3% may not sound like a lot, but if you are earning $60,000 that means you get an additional $1,800 in savings. It is like an automatic 3% raise. It is like a bonus. The astonishing thing is that millions of Americans do not take advantage of it.

Here is an example. Assume Beth works for a company with a 100% matching contribution in her 401(k) plan, up to 3% of salary. Below is the amount of her salary she would save each year towards retirement:

Employee Savings	+	100% Employer Match	=	Total Percentage Of Salary Saved
0%	+	0.0%	=	0.0%
1%	+	1.0%	=	2.0%
2%	+	2.0%	=	4.0%
3%	+	3.0%	=	6.0%
4%	+	3.0%	=	7.0%
5%	+	3.0%	=	8.0%
6%	+	3.0%	=	9.0%
7%	+	3.0%	=	10.0%

Looking at the table above, note that every time Beth saves 1% more of her income (up to 3%); her total savings grow by double that…up to a total of 6%. Also, note that once Beth maxes out on the employer match, her savings go up by her contribution amount alone. So…if Beth saves 7% of her income in this example, she will get the 3% matching contribution, and have 10% of her pay put into the 401(k) plan.

Note that Beth's take home pay is only reduced by the 7% she puts in the plan. The matching 3% from the employer goes straight into Beth's retirement account. It is a very good deal for Beth! It is even better, since Beth can now invest these savings. I will talk about that below.

Finally, 3% of pay may not sound like a lot…but over time it can add up to thousands and thousands of dollars. I cover that in the chapter titled 'You Work For Your Money – Make Money Work For You!' If Beth earns $70,000 per year, that 3% employer match is $2,100 per year. Over time, that could grow to $100,000 or more! So these are very important dollars.

Some businesses match a percentage of pay up to a certain point. Here is a common example: Assume a hospital with a 403(b) plan offers to match 50% of the first 6% of pay that is saved in Jeff's 403(b) plan. Here is a table showing how much Jeff would save in this plan:

Employee Savings	+	50% Employer Match	=	Total Saved
0%	+	0.0%	=	0.0%
1%	+	0.5%	=	1.5%
2%	+	1.0%	=	3.0%
3%	+	1.5%	=	4.5%
4%	+	2.0%	=	6.0%
5%	+	2.5%	=	7.5%
6%	+	3.0%	=	9.0%
7%	+	3.0%	=	10.0%

Note that every time Jeff saves 1% of his income in the 403(b) up to the 6% match, his total savings go up by 1.5%! You should also realize that if Jeff saves less than 6% of his income in this example, he will be giving up free money from his employer. So, Jeff should save at least 6% of his pay in this plan. Once Jeff saves 6% of his income, and maxes out the employer match, his savings amount will grow by the amount he puts in the plan. So if Jeff saved 7% of his income in the 403(b), his total savings in this example would be 10% of his income, with the other 3% coming from his employer.

What if you change jobs after saving money in a 401(k) or 403(b) plan?

You have two choices with the money in an existing 401(k) or 403(b) account. You can either:

- Keep your money in your former employer's plan (as long as you have at least $5,000 in the plan), or
- Transfer the money over into a new 401(k) plan or IRA.

You also have the option of withdrawing the money. But you should not do that. First, you need to save it for retirement, and will be giving up all the compound interest you would have earned if you withdraw it. Second, if you withdraw money from a 401(k) or 403(b) plan before age 59 ½ you will be subject to a 10% early withdrawal penalty, in addition to the regular income taxes you would owe.

Note: If you decide to transfer money from one retirement account to another, be sure that you **don't let the check be written to you**. The check has to be written to go directly into the new account. There is no grace period for putting the money into the new account. If it does come to you rather than the new account, you will be charged the income tax and the 10% early withdrawal penalty.

If you choose to keep your money in your former employer's plan, then there are also a couple of requirements. First, you have to have at least $5,000 in your account. If you have less than $5,000 in the account, your employer may require you to roll it over into an Individual Retirement Account, or 401(k) or 403(b) if you have a one with your new employer. Second, you have to be younger than the plan's normal retirement age (usually 65) to leave money in a former employer's retirement plan.

The next step is to understand how 401(k) and 403(b) plans work in terms of investing.

A 401(k) or 403(b) plan will offer you a choice of investments (usually between three and ten choices.) You choose which investments you want to put money in, and in what proportion. For instance, a 401(k) might offer the following choices:

- Growth Stock Fund
- Growth and Income Fund
- International Stock Fund
- Long Term Bond Fund
- Short Term Bond Fund
- Money Market Fund

These funds have managers who invest the money from investors in companies for you. The advantage is that you are instantly diversified. All of your money is not in just one or two stocks, but probably 50 or more. So even if one of those 50 stocks went down to $0, your losses would be minimal, since you would have a small proportion of your money invested in it.

To start, I suggest choosing one or two or three funds in which to invest. You should invest some money in a fund that invests in stocks, and then decide how much each pay period you want to go into that fund. Here is a brief description in general of these funds. Note that your particular fund may be somewhat different and you need to read about it before investing.

Growth Fund: Invests primarily in stocks.

- Risk: Stocks are volatile, and can go down as well as up – sometimes sharply in a short period of time. You can lose some or a great deal of the money you invest.
- Reward: Over long periods of time, stocks are likely to do well, and hopefully will outperform inflation.

Growth and Income Fund: Invests primarily in stocks, with some money either in bonds, which pay interest and/or stocks that pay dividends.
- Risk: Same as Growth Fund, except that bonds do well when interest rates go down, and lose money when interest rates climb. Dividends are not guaranteed, but produce income that can offset losses or add some to gains.
- Reward: Similar to Growth Fund, except that bonds can do well if interest rates are high and decline.

International Stock Fund: Invests in companies and countries outside of the United States, with some money potentially invested in the United States as well.
- Risk: Countries and their economies are each subject to various political and economic risks. If the dollar goes up against another nation's currency, it will cut the gains or add to the losses of the fund.
- Reward: Sometimes stocks in other countries outperform investments here in the United States. If the dollar declines against a foreign currency, investments in that country will see greater gains or mitigated losses.

Long Term Bond Fund: Invests in bonds (debt) of companies or governments, usually 7-30 years in length.
- Risk: If interest rates rise, these funds can go down and you can lose a significant amount of the money you invested.
- Reward: If interest rates decline, you have the potential to make some money. Some financial studies suggest that long term bonds have similar volatility to stocks, but less return. That suggests that these may not be the best investments.

Short Term Bond Fund: These invest in bonds (debt) of companies or governments, usually 30 days to two years in length.
- Risk: If interest rates rise, these funds can go down in value, but less than the Long Term Bond Fund.
- Reward: If interest rates decline, you can make some money, but not nearly as much as in the Long Term Bond Fund.

Money Market Fund: These funds invest in short term securities and earn interest, usually at low rates. They are not guaranteed to hold their value, but most firms try to hold the price to $1.00 per share.

- Risk: These funds usually pay very low rates of interest, and you may lose money compared to inflation. Inflation is the tendency of prices to rise over time. For instance, if inflation is at 3.5% and this fund only earns 0.5%, you would lose purchasing power equal to 3%. (3.5% inflation–0.5% interest = 3% loss in purchasing power.) Over time that can be a big loss, at three percent per year. In just ten years you would lose about 1/3 of your money's value.
- Reward: These funds are likely to be stable in terms of price, so that they do not fluctuate up and down like stocks and bonds.

How much should I invest in stocks?

There are many, many strategies and ideas. As this is an introductory book in financial planning, I will share one with you. One rule of thumb that is easy to remember when considering investing is to take your age, subtract it from 100, and invest the remainder in stocks. So, if you are 25 years old, take 75% of your money and invest it in funds that invest in the stock market. Invest the rest in either cash or short-term bonds. Taking this approach, you could adjust your portfolio every five years or so. This is only one idea of many. You can do all kinds of internet searches for investment suggestions.

How valuable might this advice be to invest early and often into a retirement plan? Look at the chart below. Assume you start saving $5,000 per year, and increase the dollar amount you save by 5% each year. (In Year 2, you would save $5,250 ($5,000*1.05 = $5,250)). Assume you could earn 7% per year in the account. In just 35 years, you would have $1,380,000! You would be a millionaire!

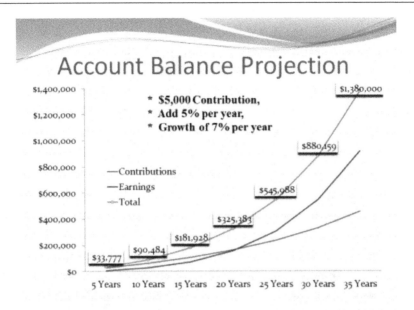

That's the power of compound interest! So, start saving <u>now</u>.

My suggestion is to start contributing at least 10% of your income into a 401(k) or 403(b), and increase the percentage each year as you get raises. It is vital that you start immediately. **Starting this now could be worth hundreds of thousands of dollars to you – that is not an exaggeration.** I discuss this more in the chapter on Making Money Work For You!

Pensions

Some employers, especially governmental employers such as school districts, may offer a pension. A pension is an offer to pay a retiree an annual income. It is typically a percentage of your final salary to you when you retire, typically if you stay five years or more. The basic formula is:

# of Years of Service X Final Salary X a percentage of Salary

Here is an example: If you work as a public school teacher for 30 years and have a final salary of $90,000 (in thirty years) and the State uses a percentage of 2%, you will have an annual pension of:

30 years x $90,000 x 0.02 = $54,000

This means you will be paid $54,000 per year after you retire until you die.

Many employers that offer a pension use an average final salary of the last three or four or five years in the calculation. Pensions can be very good if you stay with an employer for many years. Pensions are less common now, but if your employer is offering one, they can be very valuable.

One downside of pensions is that they do not pay much if someone does not stay long. For instance, assume you work as a teacher for only seven years, and quit to raise children. Later, you do something else for a career. Assume your final salary was $60,000. Your pension would only be

$$7 \text{ years} \times \$60,000 \times 0.02 = \$8,400 \text{ per year}$$

You would not receive it until you retired in your 60's.

Action Items for this chapter:
1) **If you are offered a 401(k) or 403(b) <u>always</u> contribute at least enough to get the employer match.**
2) **Save at least 10% of your income towards retirement each year. Increase that percentage each year as you receive pay increases.**
3) **Consider investing some money in stocks through investment funds offered in the plan.**

Chapter 11

Life Insurance

I have written this book primarily for college graduates. So, why would I include a chapter on life insurance, when you, dear reader, are most likely not yet old? The reason is, tragically, sometimes even young adults die. In fact, some college students died at my school in a car wreck during the semester I was writing this book. It is awful, but it does happen.

Insurance is designed to protect against a catastrophic loss. It is a terrible loss emotionally, psychologically and to friends and family members when someone dies early. It is a potentially catastrophic loss of income financially to family members as well. So, you need life insurance to protect those you love if the unexpected happens.

The primary purpose of life insurance is to replace income that is lost due to premature death. This means that you need to replace the income you would have earned if you die while in your working years. Recent college graduates have most of their working years ahead of them. This means that you may need a high amount of life insurance. Unfortunately, most Americans are vastly underinsured for life insurance purposes. According to some estimates the average American only has about $125,000 of life insurance. If you are married, or plan to be, the amount of life insurance you need is between 12 – 15 times your gross incomes. That means depending on your income, you may need $700,000–$1,000,000 or more of life insurance coverage. Employer-provided life insurance may provide some of this, but probably not all of it. You will need to buy some life insurance on your own.

There are different types of life insurance policies. There are two types of life insurance I recommend for most college graduates:
- Annual Renewable Term (ART) life insurance, and
- Level Term life insurance.

Other types of life insurance are called cash-value policies. They are much more expensive, and complicated. These are policies that build up cash within the policy – but most of them are expensive in terms of the monthly premium. The majority of them also have high costs charged by the insurance company. Because of that, I recommend either Annual Renewable Term policies or Level Term policies to recent college graduates.

Annual Renewable Term (ART)

Annual Renewable Term (ART) policies have low premiums for most applicants whose ages are in the 20's or 30's. A premium is the cost you pay to the insurance company to keep the policy in force. The premium reimburses the insurance company an amount of money to cover the risk of death, at each age, as well as to cover administrative costs and a small profit. In an ART policy, the cost of the policy, the premium, will rise slightly each year. These types of life insurance policies work well until a person reaches age 60 or so. At that point, the costs start to rise faster each year, as the risk dying starts to go up due to health problems like cancer and heart disease.

Annual Renewable Term policies typically have a set 'Face Value.' Face value is the amount of money the insurance company will pay to the beneficiary or beneficiaries if the insured dies while covered. For most ART policies, this amount does not change as long as the policy remains in force. So, for instance, if you purchase a $500,000 ART policy, it will pay out $500,000 when the insured dies, regardless of whether that is in one year, or twenty years. Of course, a down-side to that is inflation over time will erode the value of the $500,000. As prices rise over the years, the $500,000 will be able to purchase less and less. One way to minimize this is to get an ART policy either with a **Guaranteed Insurable** clause, or a **Cost-of-Living rider**.

A guaranteed insurable clause allows the insured to purchase each year (typically for five to ten years) an additional amount of insurance in the same policy without any medical exams, etc. A cost-of-living rider similarly allows the insured to purchase an amount of insurance to offset inflation each year, also under the same terms of the policy. Of course, if you do add some more life insurance to the policy under either of these provisions, you will have to pay a slightly higher premium, since you will be buying more insurance. The additional cost is typically minimal, though.

Annual Renewable Term policies terminate at a contractually set age – most at 70 – 75 years of age. This means that if you live to that age and keep the policy that long, when you reach that age, the policy will simply cease to exist. Some people think this makes term policies a waste of money, since they may never pay out. However, if you recognize that the primary purpose of life insurance is to replace income that is lost (that would have been earned) if you were to die early, then you can see that by age 70, there are few if any, working years' income left to replace. So, this policy is a good one. It frees more of your income due to its relatively low costs, for you to save, invest, and meet the general costs of daily life.

It is critical, if you get an ART policy, to make sure there is a provision in the contract that states that it is **Guaranteed Renewable**. This is very different from the 'Guaranteed Insurable' clause referred to above. A Guaranteed Renewable clause means that each year, you, the insured, are guaranteed to have the ability to renew the policy at the pre-agreed to premium costs, under the original terms of the policy, *in the health you were in when the policy was first issued*. Without this clause, the insurance company could take into account future health issues and dramatically raise the cost, or even cancel the policy.

If you are in good health, a large ART policy may be very affordable. Many times large policies–$500,000 or more–can be bought for less than $50 per month in premiums prior to middle age.

Level Term Policies

Level-term policies are life insurance policies that do not rise in cost. The premium stays level as long as the life insurance policy remains in force. Level term policies typically cost a little more in the first few years, and cost much less later, compared to ART policies. Most people should get a long-term level-term life insurance policy (25 to 30 years), rather than a short-term one. The reason is that when a level-term policy ends, you have to completely reapply for life insurance coverage.

Early in life, it is typically fairly easy to qualify for a level term policy, since most people in their 20's and 30's are healthy. However, as people age, their health declines, and the cost rises to be insured by a new policy. In cases where a person has had a significant health event, the insurance companies may not even be willing to cover a person for life insurance purposes. So, it is important

77

to get a long-term level-term policy in your 20's or 30's, which covers you for as long as possible during working years.

The good thing about level-term policies is that their premiums remain the same...they are level...every month, for the entire time the contract is in force.

When applying for life insurance, regardless of the type, it is very important to be truthful about both your own health, and your family's when asked about your health history. Some people think if they are dishonest about their health or family's health, it will not hurt them. This is not so. First, insurance companies have a vast database called the Medical Information Bureau. If you, or any relative, have ever visited any physician, any medical facility, or been prescribed any medication, the insurance company will be able to find out that information. Second, misstating facts on a life insurance application may be considered fraud. You can be found both civilly and criminally liable for fraud if the insurance company decides to pursue the matter.

Third, the insurance company can simply cancel the policy within two years of its issuance, if it finds out about any incorrect medical claims on the life insurance application. If the insured died within that time period, the insurance company could and certainly might deny payment of the face value of the policy due to fraud. This would leave loved ones who were counting on the money in a terrible position. So...be honest about your health, your parent's health, etc. when applying for life insurance. It is also simply the right thing to do.

Beneficiary designations were discussed in the chapter about Employee Benefits. Just a reminder...beneficiaries are persons who you name to inherit the life insurance proceeds if the insured person dies while being covered. It is <u>vital</u> in any life insurance contract to <u>name</u> beneficiaries with specificity. Do not use words such as "my spouse" or "my child". Those are much too vague. Unfortunately, sometimes people get divorced, for instance. Instead, if your spouse's full name is Joshua Blaine Earnest, you should list Joshua Blaine Earnest as the beneficiary, (instead of just 'my spouse'). It is fine to identify him as your spouse after specifically naming him. (Many beneficiary forms ask for the relationship of the beneficiary to you.) In addition, consider adding the beneficiary's Social Security number. That keeps someone else named 'Joshua Blaine Earnest' from successfully claiming the proceeds. Do not ever name 'My Estate' as beneficiary, or leave the beneficiary line blank. If you leave the line blank the life insurance proceeds are likely to be paid to your estate. In either case, a court will have to determine where the proceeds go, and this will both delay payment and add probate expenses that were unnecessary. It will also add complication for your loved ones when they are already grieving.

A <u>primary</u> beneficiary is someone who will receive the life insurance proceeds if you die while covered, so long as the primary beneficiary is alive at the insured's death. If you have more than one primary beneficiary, you will need to list the percentage you would like each to receive. For instance, if you have two siblings who you would like to be primary beneficiaries, you need to list them both with the percentage you would like each to receive. The percentages must add up to 100%. Be sure to list primary beneficiaries by specific name, Social Security number, and relation. For example: 'my wife, Jennifer Gomez, Social Security number 555-66-5757.'

A contingent beneficiary is someone who will receive the life insurance proceeds if you die while covered, and the primary beneficiary is not alive at that time. For instance, you might list your wife, Alyssa Montgomery, as the primary beneficiary. You might list your parents, Jeff Davidson and Elizabeth Davidson as contingent beneficiaries. This would mean that if your wife predeceased you, or if you died together, your parents would receive the life insurance proceeds. Just as for primary beneficiaries, if you have more than one contingent beneficiary, you will need to list the percentage you would like each to receive. The percentages must add up to 100%. Be sure to list contingent beneficiaries by specific full name, Social Security number, and relation as well.

Note: The discussion above regarding beneficiaries also applies to bank accounts. Be sure to have beneficiaries updated on these accounts as well.

How to Get The Best Deal in Life Insurance

If you are wondering whether there is a way to get a good deal on life insurance, there is! You can buy in bulk. Think about how much money people save by buying in bulk at warehouse stores like Sam's Club and Costco. You can do something similar to that with life insurance. Many companies will give premium discounts if a large life insurance policy is purchased. Large policies save companies money, because some expenses (website design and administration, back office operations, phone support, etc.) are fixed costs. You can check with your life insurance company, but many give premium discounts (price breaks) at face values of $500,000; $750,000 and $1,000,000. What this means, for instance, is that a $500,000 life insurance policy may not be twice as expensive as a $250,000 policy. It may cost less than twice the cost of the $250,000 policy.

Buying large policies also saves money since you will not have to buy smaller policies to cover things like car loans, mortgage payments, credit card debt or student debt, etc. Unless those insurance policies are free (some credit cards offer nominal life insurance at no extra cost, for instance), you should turn them down. They tend to be very expensive for the coverage offered, compared to large policies from reputable companies.

Some good life insurance companies include, but are not limited to, Northwestern Mutual Life Insurance Company, USAA, and Amica. I would advise you to compare not just costs, but also the financial worthiness of life insurance companies before buying policies. These contracts are likely to be long-term. You need a company that will be financially sound in good economic times and bad if a tragic early death of the insured occurs. Before buying life insurance, ask for the company's ratings from A.M. Best for the last ten years. A.M. Best rates companies on their financial condition. You want a company that has been rated 'A+' or 'A' for each of those ten years. This demonstrates financial strength over a long period of time.

If you have children under age 18, you need to have a will made, that lists Guardians, in the event of your untimely demise. A Guardian is a person listed that is responsible for raising your children if you die while they are minors. You can either hire an attorney, or buy a software package, such as WillMaker by Quicken to make a will. Be sure to talk about guardianship with the person or persons you are considering so that you know they would be willing to care for your children if a tragedy occurred.

Be sure that the life insurance beneficiary flows with your guardian selection. For instance, assume you are married to Jennifer Hernandez Gomez. If you both die, you want her parents, George and Melissa Hernandez to take care of your children. Then you would list Jennifer Gomez as your Primary Beneficiary in the life insurance policy. This means that if you die, Jennifer would be paid the proceeds of the life insurance policy. You would list Jennifer's parents, George Hernandez and Melissa Hernandez, as Contingent beneficiaries. This means that if Jennifer was not alive when you died, her parents would be paid the life insurance proceeds. You would want your will in this case to state that your wife, Jennifer Gomez, is the Guardian of your children if you die, but that if she does not outlive you, that her parents, George and Melissa Hernandez, would be contingent Guardians of your children. This way, the children are taken care of, in terms of someone that you would trust to raise them, and they are also taken care of financially, since the life insurance would be paid to support them.

Action Items:
1. **Calculate the amount of life insurance you need.**
2. **Take out a large policy to cover that need.**

3. For Annual Renewable Term polices, make sure they are Guaranteed Renewable and Guaranteed Insurable.
4. For Level Term policies, take out the longest policy you can...30 or more years if possible.
5. Name beneficiaries with specificity in the policy.
6. Update beneficiaries in bank accounts as well.
7. Make Sure You Have A Will.
8. If you have children, be sure to list guardians in the will.
9. Consider naming life insurance beneficiaries that line up with named guardians of minors.

Chapter 12

Automobile, Home & Renter's Insurance

This chapter covers insurance on automobiles, your home and related property. Renter's insurance is also covered in this chapter if you do not yet own a home.

Automobile Insurance

Be sure to always have liability insurance on your automobile. State law in all 50 states requires it. Liability insurance is required so that you can pay for accidents that you cause. Unfortunately, most states only require a minimal amount of insurance. You will need to purchase more than the minimum. Automobile liability policies typically show a series of three numbers like this: 30/60/25

These numbers each represent different things in terms of liability. This is what they mean, from left to right:

- The first number is the maximum liability coverage for bodily injury to one person that you have injured (in this case, $30,000).
- The second number is the maximum liability for <u>all</u> persons you have injured in an accident for bodily injury (in this example, $60,000).
- The third number is the maximum liability for property damage you have caused (in this case, $25,000).

It is critical to have adequate liability insurance, because if you cause injuries to other persons and/or their property, you will be sued for the damages. If you do not have adequate coverage, you may have to pay the difference – and that can be hundreds of thousands of dollars. I suggest a minimum liability coverage amount of $100/300/100.

That is $100,000 of bodily injury to one person, $300,000 total bodily injury liability in a wreck, and $100,000 in property damage liability coverage. The reason you need these higher liability limits is that even a couple of nights in intensive care can add up to over $100,000 of health costs due to a wreck, and that is just for one person. If your car hits an expensive car or careens into a house, the property liability could be $100,000 as well.

Insurance companies also offer coverages on vehicles in addition to the liability insurance noted above. These include collision coverage and comprehensive coverage on automobiles. Collision coverage pays to repair your car after an accident, up to its current value, less your deductible on the policy. Comprehensive coverage pays to repair your car for damage caused by events other than collision, such as hail damage. You can decide if and how much of these coverages you would like to purchase. Generally, I suggest that you strongly consider collision and comprehensive coverage as long as your vehicle is worth about $5,000 or more. Once your car depreciates below $5,000 it becomes more of a personal decision as to whether you want these coverages.

Renters and Home Insurance

According to the Federal Reserve, the single biggest asset and investment most Americans have is their home. Since this is the case, it would be a catastrophic loss to most Americans to lose their home in a calamity. Insurance on this asset is a necessity. Financial institutions that offer mortgages for the purchase of a home also require insurance on the property as a condition for the loan. They require this because if the home is destroyed they need the guarantee that the loan will be repaid, and funds from insurance provide that.

Renters Insurance:

Since many recent college graduates may be renting an apartment or rent house, I'll cover renters insurance first. The reason you need it is that if there is ever a fire, tornado, etc., the insurance company will pay you so that you can replace all your possessions. Most people do not have it, and it puts them at significant financial risk. I had a friend growing up who lived in a rent house after college. He went on vacation and an electrical short caused a fire that burned down the house. He lost everything he owned. He actually asked friends for old furniture so that he could just have a table, chairs, silverware, etc. to start over. I do not want that to happen to you.

Imagine having to buy all your clothes, furniture, jewelry, smart phones, computers, kitchen items, etc. all at once if someone next door starts a fire due to smoking in bed or engaging in some illegal activity…yeah, that really does happen. It adds up to tens of thousands of dollars. And you cannot wait for stores or online merchants to put items on sale, since you will have to replace everything at once. That is the reason you need renter's insurance. Here are some things that you need to know:

First, you should make sure your policy covers things at **Replacement Cost**. That is usually a rider on the policy. What it does is value items at full value, rather than depreciated value. For instance, a shirt might cost $50 to replace (replacement cost) but would be worth only $4 now as a used shirt (depreciated value). You would need the insurance company to pay you the replacement cost of your possessions. Otherwise, the policy is almost worthless, since most possessions depreciate substantially once bought.

Second, you should record your things in the apartment and store that digital video online or physically off-site, to prove what you own in the event of a calamity. Go drawer by drawer and room by room and describe what you are showing. For example, "I own four LL Bean long sleeve shirts that cost about $45 each." The insurance company will require an inventory 60 days after you file a claim. You can use the video both to prove what you owned, and to jog your own memory as to how many shirts, pants, shoes, pots and pans, picture frames, etc. that you owned. Most people cannot remember everything they own if they lose it all at once.

Homeowner's Insurance:

Some readers may already own a home, and most will someday, so I will cover Homeowner's Insurance next. There are different types of standardized insurance policies depending on the type of property insured. There are standardized policies for houses, condominiums, and spaces that are rented to others. Since this a basic book on financial planning, I will just address insurance on a house. Insurance on homes has four primary parts. Here is a list of what they are and what they cover:
- Coverage A provides protection on the dwelling itself.
- Coverage B protects other structures on the property.
- Coverage C provides insurance on personal property.
- Coverage D provides for loss of use.

Each of these is covered in depth below.

Coverage 'A' provides insurance on the primary structure of the dwelling itself. This section of the policy also insures materials and supplies located either on the premises or adjacent to the premises which are intended for use in its construction. It is critical that homeowners get insurance for homes which are being constructed before they are built so that construction materials are covered in the event they are destroyed or stolen.

How Much Should I Insure My House For?

Many consumers do not purchase an appropriate amount of insurance on their homes. Most people insure real property based on the amount they paid for it. The purchase price is usually an inaccurate reference point for insurance coverage. There are two reasons for this. First, when a property is purchased, the price includes the value of the land. The land itself does not need to be insured, because it cannot be destroyed. For instance, fire destroys the property, but the land remains. Similarly, a tornado can sweep a structure off of its foundation, but the land itself is still available to be used.

Second, the purchase price of real property does not always reflect the actual cost to rebuild a home. You need to purchase an amount of insurance that will allow you to rebuild the home if it is destroyed. Coverage 'A' provides insurance on a replacement cost basis. This means that insurance is provided at the cost of rebuilding the structure, and not its depreciated cost, up to the policy limits. It is critical, however, that owners cover the property for a high enough amount to rebuild the entire structure in case it is destroyed.

In order to come up with an accurate amount of insurance coverage on a home, the owner should contact builders in the area and find out approximately how much it would cost to rebuild a similar structure on a *per square foot* basis. The homeowners should then take that number and multiply it by the number of square feet of the dwelling. For example, assume a homeowner purchased a 2,200 square foot home for $250,000. Many people would just insure the home for $250,000. In this hypothetical, assume builders in the area gave an estimated cost to rebuild of $140 per square foot. If this home was destroyed, the cost to rebuild it would be 2,200 x $140 = $308,000. If the homeowner had simply used the purchase price for insurance coverage purposes, he or she would be short $58,000 in insurance coverage if the home was destroyed. This is actually quite common, and it is my hope that you will avoid that outcome with this information.

Coverage 'B' provides insurance on other structures on the property which are detached from the primary building. Examples include swimming pools and equipment, a detached garage, sheds, fences, etc. The default coverage for these structures is 10% of the coverage in Coverage 'A'. In the example above, if the homeowner bought a policy for $308,000 on her home, Coverage 'B' would be in the amount of $30,800. This policy coverage is in addition to the coverage on the dwelling itself…it does not reduce Coverage 'A', but is separate and additional coverage.

Coverage 'B' also covers property which is off the premises, but belongs to the homeowner. An example is the property that a college student takes to a dorm. If this property was destroyed in a fire, Coverage 'B' would pay for this, less the deductible on the policy. While the default percentage for Coverage 'B' is 10% of the Coverage 'A' amount, the homeowner can increase this coverage in the policy for an additional premium, if needed. Note that once a child has graduated from college or graduate school, he or she is no longer covered by the parent's homeowner's policy.

Coverage 'C' insures personal property in the dwelling. Coverage 'C' is a critical area, because most people are woefully underinsured in this area. Most people, surprisingly, have spent around 50% of the value of the home on the items within the home. This sounds incredibly high at first. But think about all of the items in a home. They were purchased over time, and so the cost was spread out. To replace all of those items, all at once, would be very high. **The default language in the policy for Coverage 'C' covers this property for Actual Cash Value. Actual Cash Value means the depreciated value of these belongings.**

To illustrate how inadequate Actual Cash Value coverage is, consider just one pair of shoes. How much could you get for your worn shoes today if you sold them? My guess is one to two dollars. But how much did they cost? $50? $100? How much would it cost to replace them? Now look at that, and multiply that across every single item in the home – the utensils in the kitchen, the bedspreads, and the lawn equipment – everything. Under Actual Cash Value, most items are valued at about 5% of their replacement cost.

Given that most homeowners have spent close to 50% of the dwelling cost on those items over time, the difference between what the insurance company would pay, and the actual cost to replace everything inside the home would likely be a catastrophic loss. In the example above, if a homeowner spent about $150,000 on all the items in the home, and it was destroyed, the home would be rebuilt, but under Coverage 'C', the owner would only get about $8,000 to replace everything inside. This lack of coverage is especially damaging financially, because Coverage 'C' includes items such as carpet, which is very expensive to replace, and yet has virtually no value once used.

The way to fix this problem is to insist upon a rider to the policy for Replacement Cost Coverage for Coverage 'C', rather than Actual Cash Value. By adding this provision, items within the home are covered at replacement cost, rather than depreciated cost, if they are damaged or destroyed. In the example above, the homeowner would be paid up to $150,000, instead of just $8,000 or so, if this rider was added to the policy. This rider is not an expensive provision, but it is <u>critical</u> that you have it. The default coverage limit for Coverage 'C' is 50% of the Coverage 'A' amount. A homeowner may reduce that percent to as low as 40%, or may raise it above 50% for an additional premium amount.

One significant problem which people have is they cannot remember all the items in a home when it is destroyed. This can cause a great amount of emotional distress. It is also a problem when filing a claim for all of those items with the insurance company. Insurance companies typically allow 60 days for an owner to file an inventory with them for items which need to be replaced. Many internet sites online allow people to write up an inventory of items and cost and store them online. However, this can be cumbersome. A more thorough way to record the inventory in a home is to take a video camera or other digital device, and record over a period of days the items in a home and their cost. For instance, a person might videotape the two pairs of Nike shoes he or she owns and verbally mention the cost of those shoes on the video. All items in a home should be recorded in this way.

Once this process is complete, the video should be stored online or a hard copy should be kept off-site from the house. Surprisingly, many people store these inventory videos in the home. If a fire or tornado destroys the home, the inventory record will be destroyed right along with it. A general rule of thumb is to keep such an inventory record at least 20 miles from the dwelling itself. This record provides proof to the insurance company that the items that were owned that must be covered by the policy. This record also provides backup information and may jog the memories of owners, regarding items purchased after the video was made. Owners should also keep a copy of the property insurance policy itself with the video, off-site, so that access to the policy in the event of a loss is easy to obtain.

Certain types of property are excluded from Coverage 'C', such as motorized vehicles, computer equipment, antiques, and jewelry above relatively low thresholds. Coverage for motorized vehicles is provided by automobile policies.

Antiques, jewelry, computer equipment and similar items of value can be covered by an endorsement to the policy with specific coverage limits.

Finally, Coverage 'D' provides for loss of use coverage. This coverage reimburses the homeowner for costs such as rent while the home is being repaired or rebuilt. The default coverage amount is 20% of Coverage 'A'. Note that the policy does not pay 20% of the Coverage 'A' amount automatically. Instead, this is a coverage limit. The homeowner would submit records of rent paid, storage costs, etc. to the insurance company for reimbursement while the home was repaired or rebuilt.

A wise addition to property insurance is an **inflation guard endorsement**. The clause will allow the policy coverage to rise each year to compensate for inflation over time. Without this feature, property insurance would likely have inadequate limits after only a few years.

If A Loss Occurs

If a loss occurs, there are several steps that must be taken to file a claim. First, if the loss involves theft, the police must be notified, and a police report must be filed. If the claim involves a natural disaster, the insurance company must be notified of the loss. Some people mistakenly think that insurance companies will automatically know of a loss due to natural disaster, but this is not the case. The property owner is also required to take reasonable steps to protect the property after an event occurs.

For instance, if a windstorm blows a tree into the roof, the property owner must have the hole in the roof covered after the storm passes. All receipts should be kept for materials and labor, as these will be reimbursable by the policy. An inventory of the items lost must be filed with the insurance company within 60 days of the time they are notified of the loss, accompanied by a signed statement. This requirement underscores the value of recording the items in a home, which was discussed above.

Several other provisions, not listed in sections A-D above, are also common to policies, or may be added by the policyholder. They include:
- Debris removal,
- Extensions for trees, shrubs and plants, and
- Ordinance or law provisions.

Debris removal provisions provide coverage to remove debris from the premises in the event of a loss. Debris may include trees, dust, limbs, or other property that has blown onto the owner's land, such as insulation from homes destroyed by tornadoes. It even includes ash if the loss is due to volcanic eruption. Extensions for trees, plants, etc. are provided in insurance policies to pay for replacement of these items when they are destroyed by a covered event.

Adding **Ordinance or law coverage** is important for home insurance. You should realize that replacement cost coverage of the dwelling means coverage for similar items. For instance, if a certain type of electrical wiring was used which is no longer allowed by a building ordinance, or if fire suppression systems are now required, replacement cost coverage does not include any additional costs for changes in building codes for items such as these. An Ordinance or law provision does cover those increased costs. The default ordinance and law insurance amount is 10% of Coverage 'A' in the policy. However, owners can increase this coverage in a policy to 25%, 50%, 75% or even 100% of Coverage 'A' limits for a higher premium.

Finally, you should know that **floods are not covered in property insurance policies. A separate flood policy must be purchased for this coverage.** Purchasers of real estate should find out if a property is in or out of a 100 year or 500 year flood plain. Floods are usually catastrophic events when they impact structures. Many times, losses are equal to the property value, even when waters are only a few inches deep. I strongly advise you to purchase flood insurance on real property. This insurance covers the structure for up to $250,000 and possessions for up to $100,000. Under current law, these are the highest limits available in flood policies.

Action Items:
1) **If renting, get renters insurance. Make sure it covers items at replacement cost.**
2) **If you own a home, make sure the policy covers possessions (Coverage 'C') at Replacement Cost Value.**
3) **Consider purchasing additional coverage for items like jewelry, firearms, business equipment, etc.**
4) **Consider adding an Inflation Rider to the policy to add coverage each year as building costs rise.**
5) **Consider adding additional 'Ordinance or Law' coverage to your home policy.**
6) **Record items in your apartment or home and store that digital record online or at least 20 miles away.**
7) **Get flood insurance, even if the home is not in a flood zone.**

PART IV: SAVING & INVESTING

Chapter 13

Save, Save, Save

Go to the ant, you sluggard, and consider its ways. It has no commander, no overseer or ruler. Yet it stores its provisions in summer and gathers its food at harvest. Proverbs 6:6-8 (NIV)

Using the strategies of budgeting and debt reduction in the previous chapters opens the door to saving money for all kinds of things. College graduates, like many Americans, may not be particularly skilled at saving money. It is vital now, and for your future that you do so. What I hope you will see is that you have a choice: you can spend now, and have no security at all financially every month, or you can save money, and "spend later." *I have found that people who save money have greater emotional security* along with the financial security, because they are not living month-to-month. They also intuitively know they are doing the right thing for themselves, and/or their families.

The good news is that using the skills of budgeting will lead to less spending and thus, more saving, because you will just be more aware of your costs of purchases. The question is how much to save.

I suggest saving a minimum of 10% of your pay towards retirement as soon as you have your first job. I suggest 10% because it is easy to remember, and is a good starting point. Many employers will add to that with a matching contribution in a retirement plan up to 6% of pay. Many employers offer a 401(k) plan or a 403(b) plan. I discussed these in an earlier chapter. To briefly review, in these plans, the employer will typically offer a matching contribution if you have them automatically take money out of your paycheck each pay period and have it deposited in the plan. A common match is a 50% matching contribution up to 6%. What this means is that if you make a 6% contribution to the plan, the employer will match 50% and deposit it, too. Thus, you would get an extra 3% in the retirement plan. (Your 6% + 3% from the employer = 9%).

Remember, you do not have to work harder, or do more, to get that 3%. You just have to deposit money towards retirement in the plan – something you need to do anyway. Yet millions of Americans do not participate in employer sponsored retirement plans. Do not make that mistake. Of course, you should check with your employer and save whatever will maximize the matching contribution, as my 3% example was just an illustration.

Have savings come out of your paycheck or bank account automatically, as I mentioned in Chapter 3. This does two things. First, you will not really miss the money, because it is taken out ahead of time before you are paid. Second, it keeps you from having to decide whether you want to save money every time you are paid, because it is just done automatically. Otherwise, you will have some expense and likely decide not to save that money, and that will become a repeating pattern.

As you get pay raises, take half of the raise, and put it into your retirement savings. If you get a 4% raise, add 2% to the percentage of salary you are saving. For example, if you were saving 10% of your salary for retirement, and get a 4% raise, increase your retirement contribution to 12%. Do this every year that you get a pay increase. The most important thing to do is to start. If you are not saving now, start this week. Again, **the biggest obstacle to financial success is procrastination.**

Action Items:
1) **Save at least 10% of your gross income each pay period towards retirement.**
2) **Make your savings <u>automatic</u>.**
3) **Increase your savings rate <u>each</u> <u>year</u> as you get raises.**
4) **Start immediately. Do not wait to save your income.**

Chapter 14

You Work For Money - Make Money Work For You!

"Compound interest is the 8th wonder of the world." -*Albert Einstein*

"...whoever gathers money little by little makes it grow."
Proverbs 13:11 (NIV)

O ne of the <u>core</u> keys to financial success is saving money...and saving it early. In Chicago, there is a saying, due to corruption in politics: "Vote early and often." To summarize this chapter, "Save early and often." Most of the students I teach are amazed at the difference just a few years of savings can make.

Let's start off with an analogy. Some of you have probably built a snowman in the front yard. The base of the snowman is the hardest part. You start off with a small ball, and roll it over and over and over again across the lawn. You might roll it 10 times. At the end, it might be soccer ball sized or a little bigger. Then you turn it around facing fresh snow, and roll it just one more time, and it grows in size a bit. In just one or two more rolls, you have to get help to push it just one more complete turn, because of all the snow added in that last roll.

Compound interest is like that. It is interest upon interest upon interest. And the first ten to fifteen years, it grows gradually. But then, it starts to grow much faster with each passing year. Here is an example: If you have $10,000 and earn 7% each year, you will have in one year, $10,700. (7% of $10,000 is $700). But in two years you will have $11,449, instead of just $11,400. The reason is the $700 earned the first year also earns 7% and thus you have an additional $49. It isn't a lot of money…yet. But check out the graph below at 7% growth per year:

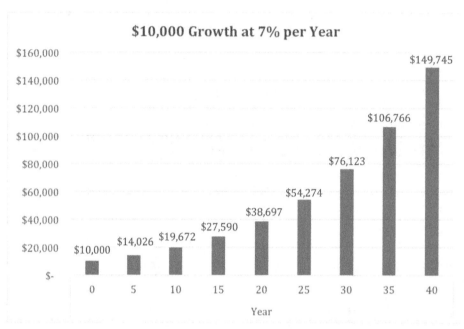

$10,000 Growth at 7% per Year

There is a lot to present in the chart and numbers above. First, look at your account after five years. With compound interest, you would have over $14,000…that's over $4,000 growth on your original $10,000 deposit. Second, it takes about 10 years **from the start**, to (almost) double your money, from $10,000 to $19,672, at 7% per year. But look what happens after that: Five years after that, you have almost $8,000 more in Year 15 than in Year 10. That is the power of compound interest. And it only grows more powerful after that!

20 years after your original investment you would have almost $39,000… that is almost **four times** the amount of your original investment of $10,000.

30 years after your original investment you would have over $76,000… more than **7½ times** your original investment of $10,000.

And 40 years after your original investment you would have almost $150,000…more than 15 times your original investment of $10,000.

Note that the time to earn each successive $10,000 is shorter and shorter and shorter. In fact, after Year 40, at 7% interest, you would earn an amount greater than the original investment ($10,000) in interest in just one year. That is the power of compound interest. It is amazing.

Second, look at that graph and look at how it gets steeper and steeper over time. That means that money is working for you – it is money earning money.

The money grows faster and works harder and harder as the years go by.
Look how fast the account grows between Year 35 and Year 40. It grows by
almost $43,000 **which is more than four times the original investment** of
$10,000.

A key thing to recognize is that many, many people put off saving money.
Another way to look at this is to realize that if you put off saving money by just
five years, you would end up with the balance at Year 35, instead of Year 40.

Put another way, by waiting just five years to save the original $10,000 it
would cost you $43,000. Would you rather have $150,000 or $107,000? Start
saving money as soon as you have a full-time job for retirement! Do NOT
put it off!

Compound Interest Applied to Mortgages:

Now, let's apply that same concept to mortgages. Most people
want to buy a home someday, and most people get a 30-year,
fixed-rate mortgage. This means the interest rate is fixed for
the life of the loan. That is OK. However, I want to point out
the high interest costs on these loans, and ways you can reduce
that cost.

Let's assume you borrow $200,000 to buy a house. (The average
price of a home in the United States is close to that amount.) If
you have a 30-year loan at 5% interest, here is some information
for you to consider:

First, look at the graph below. It shows how much interest you would pay
on the loan I just mentioned, and how much you would pay on a 20-year or
15-year loan instead.

Total Interest Paid on a 30, 20 & 15 Year Home Loan
($200,000 loan at 5% interest)

You would pay over $186,000 in interest on a 30-year, $200,000 mortgage. You would pay less than $117,000 on the same loan if you paid it off over 20 years. And you would only pay $84,685 in interest on a 15-year mortgage of the same loan. Here is a chart showing you how much you could save in interest payments by paying off a home loan faster than 30 years:

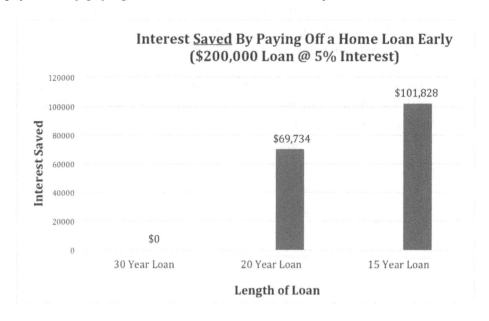

Interest Saved By Paying Off a Home Loan Early
($200,000 Loan @ 5% Interest)

You would pay over $186,000 in interest on a 30-year, $200,000 mortgage at 5% interest per year. You would pay less than $117,000 on the same loan if you paid it off over 20 years...**saving you almost $70,000 in interest! By paying off the loan in 15 years, you would pay only $84,685 in interest on the same loan....saving you almost $102,000 in interest compared to the 30-year loan!**

Here is how it works, and how you can save tens of thousands, and potentially over $100,000 in interest payments, on your home:

First, the payment of principal and interest on this loan is $1,073.64 per month. Principal is the portion of the payment that goes to repay the original loan, and interest is the amount charged by the bank. Also, the real out-of-pocket cost of the home is much more than just $1,073.64. The real monthly check is likely to be around $2,000 per month, give or take about $100. The reason is that homeowners also must pay property taxes, and property insurance. Those two items are expensive and mandatory, and are added to the monthly payment of principal and interest. I tell my classes that it is a P.I.T.I. (Principal, Interest, Taxes, Insurance) that homes are so expensive!

When you are looking to buy a home, you can estimate your monthly home mortgage payment this way: A good rule of thumb for a 30-year loan is that your monthly payment can be estimated to be roughly 1% of the loan amount, (assuming you are not paying off a large portion of the home's value with the down payment.) In this case, 1% of $200,000 is $2,000. So, your actual monthly payment is likely to be around $2,000 per month for this house, including principal, interest, property taxes and insurance.

Let's assume you buy the home with a $200,000 loan at 5% for 30 years, and that your real total monthly payment is $2,000 per month. Here is how much, over time, you might pay in principal, interest, property taxes and property insurance, and total payments towards the home:

	Principal	Interest	Property Taxes & Insurance	Total Cost
Year 1:	$2,951	$9,933	$11,116	$24,000
Year 5:	**$16,342**	$48,076	$55,582	$120,000
Year 10:	**$37,315**	$91,522	$111,163	$240,000
Year 15:	$64,231	$129,024	$166,745	$360,000
Year 20:	$98,774	$158,900	$222,326	$480,000
Year 25:	$143,105	$178,987	$277,908	$600,000
Year 30:	$200,000	**$186,513**	$333,487	$720,000

(Note that the figures above are estimates in regards to taxes and insurance. Also, the actual amount of your interest cost and these other costs will vary depending on your actual interest rate and the future cost of your home.)

You may find some of the numbers in the table surprising. Let's walk through them. First, Principal is the amount of the $200,000 loan you would have paid off each year. Interest is the total amount of interest you would have paid to the bank on the loan at each year in the house. Property taxes and insurance are the total amounts you would have paid for those at each year in the house. Total Cost is the total of all of these added together.

Let's look at just the first year. You would have spent $24,000 in house payments at $2,000 per month. Sadly, only about 12%...$2,951 of the $24,000 spent on the principal, interest, taxes and insurance would have gone towards repayment of the loan's principal. $21,049 paid other items: interest, property taxes, and insurance. Only $2,951 out of $24,000 spent…less than 1 1/2 month's worth of payments… would go to pay down the loan. After a year, you would still owe $197,049 on this mortgage.

The numbers are not that much better after five years in the home. The good news is that you would have paid back $16,342 of the loan, but would have spent a total of $120,000 on the mortgage, taxes and insurance. ($2,000 per month x 60 months = $120,000 total.) That means only about 13%...$16,342 of the $120,000 you spent the first five years would go towards repayment of the original loan amount of $200,000. **Over 86% of the $120,000 paid out the first five years would pay for interest, taxes, and insurance….not paying off the original loan.**

Even after ten long years in the house, only about $37,000 would go to principal, out of $240,000 spent. In fact, you would not even reach the point of repaying half of the $200,000 loan until after Year 20! (The principal repaid would only be $98,774 at the end of the 20th year.)

How can it be that it takes longer than 20 years on a 30-year loan to reach the point where even half of the original loan is repaid? The reason, of course, is compound interest. Except this time it is working against you, rather than for you. Interest is paid on the loan balance, which is high for a long time in a 30-year loan. For instance, at the end of the first year, the loan balance is $200,000 - $2,951 = $197,049. 197,049 x 5% (the interest rate) is almost $10,000 in interest per year. At the end of ten years, the loan balance is still quite high compared to the amount borrowed…over $162,000. Therein lies the clue to a way to cut some of this cost. I cannot help you with the taxes and property insurance, other than to shop property insurance around, and follow the tips in the prior chapter on homeowner's insurance. I can, however, provide some ideas to cut the interest cost on this loan.

First, **never, ever take out a mortgage loan (or any other loan) that has a pre-payment penalty.** A pre-payment penalty is a clause in which the borrower is penalized for paying a loan off early. Always reject loans with this provision. It is good to get out of debt early, and no borrower should be financially penalized for doing so.

Second, recognize that **compound interest can work <u>for</u> you in homeownership, instead of against you.** Let's take that same loan of $200,000 at 5% interest for 30 years. But this time, let's add $250.00 to our payment, and apply that to the loan principal each month. Remember that the actual total amount you will pay on this type of loan will be around $2,000 before the additional principal. So, we're adding just over 10% to our monthly cost. Our new payment of principal and interest is $1,323.64 and our total monthly payment is $2,250 instead of $2,000.

Here's how the numbers work out.

	Principal	Interest	Property Taxes & Insurance	Total Cost
Year 1:	$6,020	$9,863	$11,117	$27,000
Year 5:	$33,344	$46,075	$55,581	$135,000
Year 10:	$76,136	$82,701	$111,163	$270,000
Year 15:	$131,054	$107,202	$166,744	$405,000
Year 20:	$200,000	**$116,142**	$223,858	$540,000

Look at how adding just $250 per month changes things compared to the 30-year minimum payment of $2,000 per month. In the first year, instead of paying less than $3,000 towards the loan, you would have paid off over $6,000 of the loan, the principal. By the fifth year, instead of paying off only $16,342, you would have paid off more than twice that amount...$33,344. By the tenth year, you would have paid off more than 1/3rd of the loan, $76,136 instead of paying off only $37,315 with the original loan. In fifteen years, you would have paid off almost 2/3rds of the loan on your house...$131,054 by adding just $250 per month compared to just $64,231 in the original 30-year loan.

And...after 20 years you would own the home, free and clear! The mortgage would be paid off. That means money you had been paying for principal and interest, $1,323.64 per month, would be available for you to save or spend as you please! **That's almost $16,000 per year in extra cash flow.** You could take a vacation, save it, splurge, or possibly send your children to college.

Think about that for a minute. You only added about 10% to the mortgage payment, but paid off your home in 1/3rd less time – ten years earlier. How neat would it be to have a paid-off home ten years earlier?! That's leveraging compound interest to work for you instead of against you.

Finally, look at the total interest expense. The 30-year mortgage cost $186,513 in interest. Paying off the house in 20 years cost only $116,779 in interest...**a savings of almost $70,000.** So, not only would you be free of a mortgage payment ten years earlier, you would save almost $70,000 in interest!

Finally, let's look at the ability to pay off the loan in just 15 years. You can, if you add $508 to the original monthly payment of $2,000 per month. The new payment would be $2,508 per month. That would be an increase of about 25% over the original total monthly payment of $2,000, but would cut the repayment period **in half**! Here's how the numbers would work out:

	Principal	Interest	Property Taxes & Insurance	Total Cost
Year 1:	$9,188	$9,791	$11,117	$30,096
Year 5:	$50,889	$44,009	$55,582	$150,480
Year 10:	$116,199	$73,598	$111,163	$300,960
Year 15:	$200,000	**$84,685**	$166,759	$451,440

Look at the table above. Remember that Principal is the amount of the $200,000 loan that you would have paid off. In just five years, you would have over 25% of the house...$50,889 of the $200,000 loan would be paid off. In ten years, you would have almost 60%...$116,199 of your home paid off.

And in 15 short years, you would be a homeowner with **no mortgage payment**. You would have paid off the entire $200,000 loan. Compare that to the 30-year loan, where, after 15 years, you would have paid off only $64,231. **Instead of paying a total of $186,513 in interest over 30 years, you would only pay $84,685 – a savings of over $100,000 in interest.** That is definitely compound interest put to work for you and not against you. These numbers are actually conservative, because a 15-year loan usually has an interest rate about 0.5% lower than a 30-year loan, which means your savings in interest would be even greater.

People ask me all the time if it is better to get a 15-year mortgage or a 30-year mortgage. My answer may surprise you. I generally suggest getting the 30-year mortgage, and adding principal to it each month, even though the 15-year note would have a slightly lower interest rate. The reason I generally suggest getting a 30-year mortgage is the lower payment provides some financial flexibility. What if one month you really need that extra $508 that was going towards the principal for something? Of course, the problem is many people will then get in the habit of spending that money, instead of applying it to the mortgage payment. As I mentioned earlier, **financial planning is as much about discipline as it is about money.** Other than a true emergency, it would be prudent, I think, to pay off the mortgage early.

Here is a link to an online calculator to see how much you can save on your own home loan by adding to your monthly payment:
http://www.dynamicontent.net/dcv2/indiv_calc.php?calc=5&key=wolfecpa2

Action Items:
1) **Make money work for you. Save money now. Save every pay period. Do not put it off.**
2) **If or when you buy a home, make sure the loan does not have a pre-payment penalty.**
3) **Add money to your monthly house payment, towards the principal, every month. Try to add at least 10% of the total payment due to your mortgage payment every month. Be sure to designate the additional money as payment to the principal of the loan to pay off the home early.**

Chapter 15

Bank Accounts, Emergency Funds, & Brokerage Accounts

In this chapter, I will explain the basics of various personal savings accounts, including bank accounts, emergency funds, and brokerage accounts.

Bank Accounts

Bank accounts, such as checking and savings accounts, earn interest, usually at low rates. Savings accounts typically pay a higher rate than checking accounts. A good web site to find the financial institutions that pay higher interest rates is: www.bankrate.com.

Basically, accounts at financial institutions are usually insured by the Federal Deposit Insurance Corporation (FDIC) up to $250,000, per depositor, per bank. This means that if the financial institution goes under due to bad loans, your money would be reimbursed up to those limits. There are other rules and limits to FDIC coverage beyond the scope of this book, dealing with the number and types of accounts a person can have at a financial institution with FDIC coverage. Here is a web link for more details: https://www.fdic.gov/deposit/covered/categories.html. Since most recent college graduates will not have savings above $250,000 for several years, this is as in-depth as you need to know for now.

Certificates of Deposit (CD's) are another type of account at financial institutions. They differ from savings accounts in that they last for a specific term.

Common lengths of time are 3 months, six months, one year, two year, three year, four year and five year CD's. When a CD's term ends, it is said to have matured. Usually, the longer the term, the higher the rate of interest that will be paid to your account. Unlike checking and savings accounts, you typically cannot withdraw money from a CD without penalty until the CD matures.

Emergency Funds

It is a good idea to save the equivalent of three to six months of expenses in an emergency fund, and to consider putting them in a savings account. This is a fund to use when unexpected things happen – a car wreck or expensive car repairs, health problems that you did not expect; a layoff from work, a fire, etc. This fund can provide a financial cushion when you need it most.

Make sure you can get money out of this account without penalty whenever you need to, as emergencies usually happen suddenly and without warning.

Save according to the following schedule:
Year 1: 2% of gross income into the Emergency Fund account
Year 2: 3% of gross income into the Emergency Fund account
Year 3: 4% of gross income into the Emergency Fund account
Years 4-30: 5% of gross income into the Emergency Fund account

Brokerage Accounts

In addition to bank accounts, another place to put savings is in a brokerage account. A brokerage account is an account that allows you to invest in stocks, bonds, mutual funds, and exchange-traded funds (ETF's). Even if you do not know much about stocks or bonds, it may be a good idea to put some money into a brokerage account to invest in the stock market. Over time, the stock market has provided returns that are significantly higher than interest from a bank. The downside is that the stock market can of course, go down, and you can lose money, unlike in a bank account.

One thing I want to urge you to do is avoid investing in stocks through a brokerage account at a major bank. Banks such as Bank of America and Wells Fargo do offer brokerage accounts. Their offerings sometimes come with higher fees than other alternatives, however. Many people invest with them out of familiarity, but I would suggest choosing a brokerage firm such as Charles Schwab or Fidelity, each of which has much lower costs than major banks.

Here is the contact information for these companies:
Fidelity: 800.544.6666 www.fidelity.com

Charles Schwab: 866.855.9112   www. Schwab.com

Another option is to open an account at a firm that will invest the money for you inexpensively. One such company is: www.betterment.com

How To Open A Brokerage Account to invest in the stock market

1) Contact a brokerage firm, like Fidelity or Schwab to open the account, either online or on the phone.
2) Send money to the account either by check or electronic transfer from a bank account.
3) Once the account is open and cash is in it, choose an investment.

One easy way to get started investing is to choose either a mutual fund or an exchange traded fund (ETF) that mimics the stock market as a whole. By using this type of investment to start, you would be instantly diversified, which means you would automatically be invested in a large number of companies through this one fund. Also, some of these funds charge very low fees.

If you plan on investing relatively small amounts each month ($0 to $500 each month), I recommend a mutual fund. Exchange traded funds sometimes are less expensive, but you usually have to pay a brokerage fee to buy and sell them. Some mutual funds do not have those fees. A good starting investment might be a Vanguard Index 500 fund. This fund copies the S&P 500 (Standard & Poor's), which is an index of 500 stocks of large companies in the stock market. If you decide to invest in it, the trading symbol is VFINX. There are risks, of course, in putting money in the stock market. The account will go up and down in value, and the risk is that in a severe down market, you may lose some of your original investment. The advantage is that you may make money in the market when it goes up. This mutual fund only charges 0.17% per year. That means it would cost only $17 per year on an investment of $10,000. It would only cost $170 per year when your account reached $100,000 in size. That is very inexpensive. There are some lower cost funds, but this fund is near the bottom in terms of cost. It is well-known, and has been available since the early 1980's.

Dollar Cost Averaging

Investing money each month is a method called Dollar Cost Averaging. What that means is that sometimes you will buy when the share price is lower, due to a market decline, and sometimes higher, when the market is rising. Your average price will be the average price you paid over time.

Here is a simplified example:

Assume you invested $300.00 each month for four months in a volatile investment. The first month you bought three shares at $100 per share. The next month you bought two shares at $150 per share. The third month, the price declined, and you bought six shares at $50 per share. Finally, the last month, the price returned to the same point as the very first month...$100 per share, so you bought three shares. See the graph below.

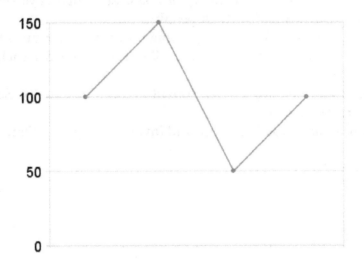

In this simplified example, over four months you would have bought 3+2+6+3 = 14 total shares, at a total cost of $300 x 4 months = $1,200. Your average cost would have been: $1,200 / 14 shares = $85.71 per share. You would have a profit at a price of $100 per share in the fourth month, even though the price of the stock was the same as the first month ($100 per share.) Certainly, dollar cost averaging does not guarantee a profit – if the price of your investment continues to decline, you will lose some money. However, it does provide a good starting point for systematic investing as you are paid each pay period.

If you get a lump sum to invest, perhaps due to an inheritance or large bonus at work, you can consider investing in an exchange traded fund (ETF). Brokerage firms usually charge a fee to buy and sell these, which is why you should not use these for small investments. For example, Fidelity charges about $8.00 every time you buy and every time you sell shares. However, some of these ETF's can be very, very inexpensive to own. One is VTI, the Vanguard Total Market Index. It only costs 0.05% per year to own. That means for a $50,000 investment, this would only cost $25 per year to own. It would only cost $50 per year for an investment of $100,000! That is just about as inexpensive as it can get in the investment world.

Action Items:
1) **Save three to six month's worth of mandatory expenses in an emergency fund.**
2) **Save emergency fund money in a bank account that you could withdraw quickly and without penalty.**
3) **Start saving 2% of gross income into your emergency fund, and increase that by 1% per year until you are saving 5% each year into this fund.**
4) **Consider opening an investment account at Fidelity, Schwab, or Betterment.com.**
5) **Use Dollar Cost Averaging and invest every pay period.**

Chapter 16

Individual Retirement Accounts (IRA's)

Individual Retirement Accounts are a great way to save towards retirement. If you do not have a retirement plan at work, an IRA may be your best retirement savings account. IRA's offer a convenient way to save money for the future. The way they work is they allow anyone earning money at a job to put some of those earnings into an IRA.

Here is the maximum amount you can deposit in an IRA in 2016:
- If you are 49 years old or younger: Up to $5,500 per year
- If you are 50 years old or older: Up to $6,500 per year

These maximum amounts will go up in future years to adjust for inflation. Feel free to type 'IRA contribution limit' into a search engine to find limits in future years.

Note that you can contribute less than the maximum amount each year. You can also put money into IRA's weekly or monthly (such as $100 per month) instead of all at once. For many people that is an easier way financially to do it. Anyone that has earned income from a job can put money into an IRA, whether or not he or she is also in another retirement plan, such as a 401(k) or 403(b) or pension.

There are two broad types of IRA's:
- Traditional IRA's
- Roth IRA's

Traditional IRA's:

Traditional IRA's allow most people to deposit money in an IRA and get a tax deduction for it. A tax deduction means that money is not subject to income tax when it is put into an IRA. So…it makes a traditional IRA a kind of tax shelter.

Here is a simplified example:

Melissa earns $60,000 per year. Ignoring other tax deductions, rules, etc., if Melissa deposits $5,500 into an IRA in 2016, her taxable income may be reduced by $5,500.

Put another way, if Melissa was in the 25% income tax bracket, she would save $1,375 in income taxes. ($5,500 IRA contribution x 25% tax bracket = $1,375 tax savings)

Money in a traditional IRA grows tax-deferred, too. This means that when the account grows over time, the money in the IRA is not taxed, as long as it is not withdrawn. To defer something means to put it off until a later date. Money in a traditional IRA's is not taxed until it is withdrawn…hopefully not until retirement a long time from now. This would give the money years to grow. When money is withdrawn from a traditional IRA, it is taxed at that time. This makes sense, since it was not taxed when it was deposited. Think about the potential growth that can occur in an IRA over time. In the chapter titled, 'You Work For Money – Make Money Work For You!' I showed how much money can grow over long periods of time.

The amount someone can deposit in an IRA is adjusted upwards for inflation every couple of years. So, in an example below, I assumed you would increase your annual traditional IRA contribution by $500 every two years.

Check out the following table, for an illustration of how much you could have, if you earned 7% per year in your IRA:

Year	IRA Contribution	Growth Each Year	Account Balance at End of Each Year
1	$ 5,500	$ 385	$ 5,885
2	$ 5,500	$ 797	$ 12,182
3	$ 6,000	$ 1,273	$ 19,455
4	$ 6,000	$ 1,782	$ 27,237
5	$ 6,500	$ 2,362	$ 36,098

6	$ 6,500	$ 2,982	$ 45,580
7	$ 7,000	$ 3,681	$ 56,261
8	$ 7,000	$ 4,428	$ 67,689
9	$ 7,500	$ 5,263	$ 80,452
10	$ 7,500	$ 6,157	$ 94,109
15	$ 9,000	$ 12,003	$ 183,474
20	$ 10,000	$ 20,686	$ 316,194
25	$ 11,500	$ 33,387	$ 510,342
30	$ 12,500	$ 51,684	$ 790,027
35	$ 14,000	$ 77,870	**$ 1,190,302**
40	$ 15,000	$ 115,081	**$ 1,759,089**

If you save in an IRA, you could have over 1.7 million dollars in 40 years (age 65 if you started at 25)! Of course, I cannot guarantee that you will have this much money. You could have more, or less, depending on how much you save, and how well your investments do. The odds are that you can do well over time if you save and invest regularly. An IRA can be set up almost anywhere…at a bank, at a brokerage firm to be invested in the stock market, or a credit union.

Can You Get A Tax Deduction For Your IRA Contribution?

If you do not have a retirement plan at work, your IRA contribution is fully tax deductible.

If you do have a retirement plan at work, such as a 401(k) or 403(b), then an IRA contribution is only tax deductible if you meet certain income limits:

In 2016, if you are single, and have MAGI (Modified Adjusted Gross Income) under $61,000 your contribution is fully tax deductible. (For most people, this is the 'Adjusted Gross Income' on your tax return.) If you earn more than that, I recommend contributing to a Roth IRA instead…see below.

In 2016, if you are married and filing a joint tax return (Married Filing Jointly), and have MAGI (Modified Adjusted Gross Income) under $98,000 your contribution is fully tax deductible. If you earn more than that, I also recommend contributing to a Roth IRA instead...see below.

Note: You cannot withdraw any money from a traditional IRA account before age 59 ½ without a 10% tax <u>penalty</u>, in addition to regular income taxes you would owe on the amount you withdrew. There are some exceptions, but I hope you will not withdraw money from these accounts. The only way to retire comfortably someday is to save regularly and not invade these accounts for other things.

Roth IRA's:

Roth IRA's allow most people to deposit money in this type of IRA. However, Roth IRA's differ from Traditional IRA's in the following ways:

1) There is no tax deduction for contributing money into a Roth IRA. This means that if you put money into a Roth IRA, it will not change the amount of income taxes you owe that year at all. That does not sound good at first. However...

2) When the money is withdrawn after age 59 ½, there are **no income taxes owed, at all! All of the money in the Roth, including the growth in the account over the years, is <u>income tax free</u> when it is withdrawn after 59 ½, under current tax law.** That is amazing. Remember the IRA table above – if that is in a Roth, the entire account is income tax free if you hold it until at least age 59 ½. I personally think Roth IRA's are the best way to save.

Note that before opening a Roth IRA, there are some income limits. If you are single, you can contribute to a Roth if your income is $116,000 per year or less. If you are Married Filing Jointly, you can contribute to a Roth IRA if your combined income is $183,000 or less in 2016. These limits rise each year with inflation. You can check the following web site for updates each year: <u>http://www.rothira.com/roth-ira-limits</u>.

However, if you fortunate enough to earn an amount above those limits, there is still a way to contribute to a Roth IRA. You have to follow these steps:

1) Open an empty **non-deductible** IRA account at the same place you either have an existing Roth or want a new Roth IRA account.

2) If you do not have a Roth IRA account open yet, open up an empty Roth IRA account at the same financial institution as the Non-deductible IRA account.

3) Deposit money (up to the contribution limits…$5,500 in 2016 for persons age 49 and under, and $6,500 for persons 50 or older in 2016) into the Non-deductible IRA account. Make sure it is not earning anything or invested in anything that changes in value.
4) About a week later, have the bank or brokerage firm transfer (convert) the money from the Non-deductible IRA account into the Roth IRA account.
5) The next year, put more money into the Non-deductible IRA account, and a week later, convert that money to the Roth IRA account. Repeat each year.

Note: If you have an existing traditional IRA account, there are additional steps and tax considerations beyond the scope of this book to convert money into a Roth. See a tax advisor or accountant in that case before converting money in a Traditional IRA into a Roth.

Information regarding both Traditional IRA's and Roth IRA's:

Only earned income can be contributed into an IRA. However, if a relative gives you a gift of money, and you earned income during the year equal to the amount of the gift, you can certainly put money from that gift into an IRA (up to the annual limits.)

Also, those annual limits are for both types of IRA's. So, for instance, you cannot put $5,500 into a Roth IRA and $5,500 into a traditional IRA in the same tax year. $5,500 is a ceiling, regardless of what type of IRA you choose.

You can make the contribution to an IRA automatic each week or month with most financial institutions. For instance, you could have the bank take $450 each month out of your checking account and deposit it into the IRA. If you cannot afford to start at that amount, begin at $100 or $200 or $300 each month, and increase it as you get raises each year.

Finally, there is an exception to the earned income rule. If you are a spouse that stays at home, you can open your own Traditional IRA or Roth IRA account and contribute to it using the employed spouse's income. This is a good rule, as it allows married adults who may be out of the workforce (such as to take care of young children) the ability to save for retirement, which they will need later.

Action Items:
1) **Open a Traditional IRA or Roth IRA account at Fidelity, Schwab, or Betterment.com.**

2) **Save money each year in either a traditional IRA or Roth IRA.**
3) **If you earn above the income limits to contribute to a Roth IRA, follow the steps below to contribute to a Roth IRA:**
    a. Open an empty **non-deductible** IRA account at the same place you either have an existing Roth or want a new Roth IRA account.
    b. If you do not have a Roth IRA account open yet, open up an empty Roth IRA account at the same financial institution as the Non-deductible IRA account.
    c. Deposit money (up to the contribution limits...$5,500 in 2016 for persons age 49 and under, and $6,500 for persons 50 or older in 2016) into the Non-deductible IRA account. Make sure it is not earning anything or invested in anything that changes in value.
    d. About a week later, have the bank or brokerage firm transfer (convert) the money from the Non-deductible IRA account into the Roth IRA account.
    e. The next year, put more money into the Non-deductible IRA account, and a week later, convert that money to the Roth IRA account. Repeat each year.

PART V: OTHER TOPICS

Chapter 17

Preparing & Filing Taxes

"Two things are certain in life: death and taxes." –Benjamin Franklin

"I want to put off the first, and minimize the second." -Andrew Schaffer

In a book about financial planning, I would be remiss to not include a chapter on taxes. I am a tax attorney by training, but don't worry…this is not some complex chapter on taxes. I just want to touch on a few points for college graduates.

W-4 Form

If you have never filled out a W-4 Form for an employer, here is what it looks like, with some sample boxes and lines filled in:

Personal Allowances Worksheet (Keep for your records.)

A Enter "1" for **yourself** if no one else can claim you as a dependent . . . . A ①

B Enter "1" if: { • You are single and have only one job; or
• You are married, have only one job, and your spouse does not work; or
• Your wages from a second job or your spouse's wages (or the total of both) are $1,500 or less. } . . B ____

C Enter "1" for your **spouse**. But, you may choose to enter "-0-" if you are married and have either a working spouse or
more than one job. (Entering "-0-" may help you avoid having too little tax withheld.) . . . . C ____

D Enter number of **dependents** (other than your spouse or yourself) you will claim on your tax return . . . . . . D ____

E Enter "1" if you will file as **head of household** on your tax return (see conditions under **Head of household** above) . E ____

F Enter "1" if you have at least $1,500 of **child or dependent care expenses** for which you plan to claim a credit . . F ____
(Note. Do not include child support payments. See Pub. 503, Child and Dependent Care Expenses, for details.)

G **Child Tax Credit** (including additional child tax credit). See Pub. 972, Child Tax Credit, for more information.
• If your total income will be less than $58,000 ($86,000 if married), enter "2" for each eligible child.
• If your total income will be between $58,000 and $84,000 ($86,000 and $119,000 if married), enter "1" for each eligible
child plus "1" **additional** if you have 4 or more eligible children. G ①

H Add lines A through G and enter total here. **Note.** This may be different from the number of exemptions you claim on your tax return.) ► H ①

For accuracy, complete all worksheets that apply. {
• If you plan to **itemize or claim adjustments** to income and want to reduce your withholding, see the **Deductions and Adjustments Worksheet** on page 2.
• If you have **more than one job** or are **married and you and your spouse both work** and the combined earnings from all jobs exceed $40,000 ($25,000 if married), see the **Two-Earners/Multiple Jobs Worksheet** on page 2 to avoid having too little tax withheld.
• If **neither** of the above situations applies, **stop here** and enter the number from line H on line 5 of Form W-4 below. }

--------------- **Cut here and give Form W-4 to your employer. Keep the top part for your records.** ---------------

Form **W-4**

Department of the Treasury
Internal Revenue Service

Employee's Withholding Allowance Certificate

► Whether you are entitled to claim a certain number of allowances or exemption from withholding is subject to review by the IRS. Your employer may be required to send a copy of this form to the IRS.

OMB No. 1545-0074

2008

1 Type or print your first name and middle initial. **FIRST NAME**   Last name **LAST NAME**   2 Your social security number 000 00 0000

3 Home address (number and street or rural route) **YOUR ADDRESS AT YOUR HOME COUNTRY**
☑ Single ☐ Married ☐ Married, but withhold at higher Single rate.
Note. If married, but legally separated, or spouse is a nonresident alien, check the "Single" box.

City or town, state, and ZIP code **YOUR ADDRESS AT YOUR HOME COUNTRY**
4 If your last name differs from that shown on your social security card, check here. You must call 1-800-772-1213 for a replacement card. ► ☐

5 Total number of allowances you are claiming (from line H above or from the applicable worksheet on page 2) 5 ____
6 Additional amount, if any, you want withheld from each paycheck . . . . 6 $ ____
7 I claim exemption from withholding for 2008, and I certify that I meet **both** of the following conditions for exemption.
• Last year I had a right to a refund of all federal income tax withheld because I had no tax liability **and**
• This year I expect a refund of all federal income tax withheld because I expect to have no tax liability.
If you meet both conditions, write "Exempt" here . . . . ► 7 ____

Under penalties of perjury, I declare that I have examined this certificate and to the best of my knowledge and belief, it is true, correct, and complete.

Employee's signature
(Form is not valid unless you sign it.) ► **(SIGNATURE)**   Date ► **(DATE)**

8 Employer's name and address (Employer: Complete lines 6 and 10 only if sending to the IRS.)   9 Office code (optional)   10 Employer identification number (EIN)

For Privacy Act and Paperwork Reduction Act Notice, see page 2.   Cat. No. 10220Q   Form **W-4** (2008)

Note that on this sample form, there is only <u>one</u> personal allowance on Line 'A' and Line 'H'. The more personal allowances you put on a W-4, the less income taxes are withheld from your paycheck. While that sounds good at first, the problem is that if too little income taxes are withheld from your paychecks through the year, you may owe a lot of money when you file your tax return, due to under-withholding. So, even if you are married or have children (dependents), I suggest just choosing one personal allowance on your W-4. If too many tax dollars are taken out of your paycheck, you can get a <u>refund</u> next year when you file your tax return! You can use that refund each tax year towards expenses, or savings. Note that on Box 3, if you are married, check the box 'Married, but withholding at the higher Single rate.'

Preparing Tax Returns

In regards to calculating income taxes, I strongly suggest using a software program such as TurboTax. There are several reasons I recommend this:

First, you can save money by just buying the software instead of hiring someone to do your taxes.

Second, you will save time. While it will take some time, especially the first time you use the software, you will save a great deal of time every year after that. The reason is that once you use the software one year to file your taxes, the next year the software copies over from the prior year many things that you would otherwise have to manually type: Your name, address, employer, spouse's name, children's names, Social Security numbers, etc. The software uses a question and answer method to help you calculate your taxes, and fills out the tax forms for you. This also saves time because you do not have to read complex tax forms.

The software saves you time in other ways. It can electronically download your tax statements from your banks, employers, etc., in many cases so that you do not have to manually key in that information each year.

Finally, I suggest using tax preparation software such as TurboTax, because different surveys through the years from Money magazine and the Wall Street Journal and others have shown that the closest accurate tax filings come from using tax software like TurboTax.

Filing Tax Returns With The Internal Revenue Service

I suggest that you file your Form 1040 income tax return <u>electronically</u> each year, rather than mailing in a paper return. The reason I urge you to do this is that electronic returns with the Internal Revenue Service (I.R.S.) have a very, very low error rate (on the part of the I.R.S.). Paper 1040 income tax returns that are mailed to the I.R.S. have a much higher error rate, because people there must manually key in all the information from the paper returns into the I.R.S. computers. The bad news is that if they make a mistake, they are not liable – you are. It may set you up for an audit one, two or three years later. It sounds terribly unfair, but that is the way the I.R.S. operates. So, to avoid that, file your 1040 return electronically. You will get an electronic confirmation from the I.R.S. that it was received…print that and keep it. Also, print out a paper copy of your 1040 income tax return and keep it in a file for at least seven years, in case of an audit or inquiry from the I.R.S.

Minimizing Taxes

Several other chapters suggest ways to reduce income taxes, including contributing to a retirement plan at work, funding an Individual Retirement Account (IRA), contributing to a Health Savings Account, and other ideas.

Keep track of all of your charitable contributions and get receipts for all of them. Items such as mortgage interest and property taxes are also potentially tax deductible. The tax software I mentioned above will help you minimize your income tax liability. Since this an introductory book on financial planning, I will keep this chapter short and end the discussion of income taxes here. But the information above will help you!

Action Items:
1) **Fill out a W-4 and choose just one Personal Allowance.**
2) **Use tax software, such as TurboTax, to prepare your 1040 Income Tax Return each year.**
3) **File your 1040 income tax return electronically with the I.R.S.**

Chapter 18

How Do I Prevent Identity Theft?

One of the challenges facing you in an interconnected world is identity theft. There are numerous ways your identity can be stolen. Someone that gains access to your accounts can charge items on a credit card, empty your bank accounts and cause not just financial harm but frustration and time as you try to fix the things that have gone wrong. The cost can be in the thousands of dollars to fix your accounts. But there are some simple things you can do to minimize the risk. Here is a list:

1) Keep your savings and checking accounts separate. Banks often allow customers to link these accounts, so that checks or debit card purchases won't be rejected. By linking the accounts, banks offer the opportunity for savings accounts to automatically 'cover' any charges on a debit card or written check. However, the risk is that someone who steals your debit card number can then empty <u>both</u> accounts. I suggest not linking the accounts. Keep only a small cushion in your checking account, and use the savings account periodically to manually transfer money to checking as you need it – but not automatically. This way, the only money a thief can get from a debit card is the money in the checking account. The savings account will be safe from being pilfered.

2) Consider using a credit card for purchases, rather than a debit card. The risk of doing this is that you will overspend and get into credit card debt…which is not something I recommend. However, if you are careful to charge only what you would have bought with a debit card, there are some advantages. First, if someone gets access to your credit

card number, you can challenge those charges with the credit card company. Those charges will be suspended while under investigation, and you will not owe money on those purchases, so long as you notified the credit card company as soon as you knew there were unusual charges on the card. This differs from a debit card, in which money is immediately drained from your account, and you have to try to get the bank to restore the funds. That process can take weeks. In addition this may cause checks that have been written to bounce. Your debit card may also be unusable since there is no money in the account. If you use a credit card for purchases, this also keeps thieves from capturing your debit card information at retailers such as Target, which was hacked in 2015.

3) When you need cash at an ATM, sophisticated thieves sometimes put a 'skimmer' – a card reader with a camera – onto the ATM machine. When you swipe your card, the skimmer reads the card number from the magnetic strip on the debit card, and the camera records your PIN when you enter it into the ATM. Robin Sidell in the Wall Street Journal suggested three strategies to minimize the risk of theft in this instance:

a. Choose ATM's that are not isolated away from view. Choose ATM's that are in a public place that make it hard for thieves to approach to install the skimmer.

b. Look at the ATM before inserting your debit card. Are there any loose items or things that look out of place? If so, go to another machine.

c. Always cover the keypad with your hand when entering your PIN, even if no one else is around. This way, if there is a skimmer, the camera on it cannot record that vital piece of information.

4) When using a debit or credit card, keep the numbers covered up when in public. Most people just lay the card on the table at a restaurant, or at a retailer, when anyone with a camera can walk by and get the number.

5) Increasingly, debit and credit cards have Radio Frequency Identification Devices (RFID's) built into them. These allow cards to be used by just waving them in front of a device that captures the information. The downside is that thieves have devices that can also capture that information, and they can do it by just walking by you in a store, or a restaurant, or any other place. To prevent this, **buy an RFID blocking wallet or card holder.**

6) **Limit the number of credit card accounts that you have.** If you close an account, ask for proof via a letter from the credit card company that the account is closed. Inactive, but open accounts are ripe for theft, and

you may not notice for some time if it is a credit card you do not regularly use.

7) **Get your credit information at least once a year from Annualcreditreport.com**. Check it over carefully and make sure accounts that are supposed to be closed are listed as such, and that your other accounts have the right balances.

8) **Make sure you have antiviral software both on your computer and your smart phone**.

Action Items:

1) Do not link checking and savings accounts.
2) Use ATM's in public places and look at them closely before using them.
3) Cover up credit and debit card numbers when using them in public.
4) Get a RFID blocking card holder or wallet for credit and debit cards.
5) Check credit at least once a year using annualcreditreport.com.
6) Keep updated antiviral software on your smart phone and computer.

Chapter 19

How Can I Lower the Cost of Buying a Vehicle?

It may seem ironic that after covering budgeting and debt management earlier in this book I would focus on buying a car, SUV, truck or minivan. However, amazing as it may sound, most people over their lives will spend more on vehicles than their homes, because cars have to be replaced several times over a lifetime. Since it is inevitable that you will need to buy a vehicle at various points in life, I wanted to share some strategies to minimize costs on these major purchases. I teach Negotiations at my university and there are some strategies you can employ when purchasing an automobile.

First, do your homework. This means you should read online sources such as Consumer Reports, which costs only $20 per year for a subscription, to find cars that are reliable and perform well. You can also read a great article on Edmunds.com regarding new car purchases. Here's the link:

http://www.edmunds.com/car-buying/10-steps-to-finding-the-right-car-for-you.html

Once you have settled on one or two models, pull up historical sales price information. One site to use is www.truecar.com. You can find the prices other people have paid for the car. Copy off this information and put it in a folder. I suggest a physical copy rather than one on a smart phone or tablet so that you can show it to the salesperson or manager on the table and reference it easily.

Next, see if there are any incentives offered by the manufacturer on the car. Check both the website of the manufacturer, and Edmunds.com. Incentives might include rebates – sometimes thousands of dollars, or low interest rate loans. Be sure to check around with your financial institution for a lower rate loan before just taking the loan from the dealer, if you are borrowing to pay for the car. The internet site, www.Bankrate.com can also provide loan rates for automobile purchases.

If you plan to trade in a car, be diligent in finding the market price of the car you are trading in to the dealership. **Search www.truecar.com, www.kbb. com, and www.ConsumerReports.com.** Copy off the information you find, then look at the dealer's website and see what a similar car with similar miles is selling for. Copy off this information and add it to your folder as well.

With all this information, now it is time to test drive the cars. Do so on a dry day…wet weather can muffle sounds and rattles. Listen to the information given to you by the salesperson, but do not succumb to any pressure to buy the car. Think about the list of items in the Edmunds.com article and look and sit in the front, rear, and third-row (if applicable) seats. Check the size of the back or trunk.

A critical thing to realize is that if you are trading in a car, you are involved in two separate negotiations. The first is the price of the new car. The second is the price the dealer will give you for your trade. In regards to the new car, always negotiate from the bottom of the True Car prices. Do not let a dealer "add on" stuff like vehicle tracking, paint sealant, or after-market items you did not want, etc. Tell them you are willing to wait on a car that comes in without all that, or to remove unwanted after-market items from the cost of the car. You can also consider a pre-negotiated price for the new car purchase from firms such as USAA. In this case, USAA guarantees the price of the car, by pre-negotiating with selected dealers. You can go to www.USAA.com to find out about this service.

Dealerships make most of their money on new car purchases from two sources…the trade-in value they offer for your existing car, and in the finance department. **When trading in a car to a dealership, negotiate from the top of the trade-in range from kbb.com, Consumer Reports, etc.** Consider getting quotes from places like CarMax to negotiate as well. Be sure to copy off all of this information and take it to the dealership. If you feel you are not getting a fair offer, go to another dealer. One key thing: By trading in a car, you are reducing the sales tax on the vehicle you are buying. For instance, if your state has a 6% sales tax, and you are buying a new car priced at $30,000, with a trade-in worth $10,000 then the sales tax is only applied to the difference…$20,000. That $10,000 trade-in would save you $600 in sales tax. This only happens if you trade in the car, rather than selling it to another company or party. So, be sure to factor in the sales tax savings when considering whether or not to sell your existing car yourself or to a different dealership than the one selling you the new car.

Buying a new car takes time, and is stressful. Dealerships know this, and try to wear you down emotionally before closing the deal. They know many people just capitulate in the finance office, where the paperwork is finalized, because they are tired. **Do not let your guard down.** The person in the finance office is typically paid by commission to sell you all kinds of things: extended warranties, key replacement insurance, dent and scratch coverage, theft-tracking (for an extra cost, of course), and on and on. Typically, you should turn down all of this. Double check the paperwork before you sign anything, as mistakes are made – whether innocently or not.

Then…enjoy your new car! **Do not forget to update your auto insurance.** Remove the vehicle that was previously on the policy, and add the new vehicle.

Saving Money on Vehicle Maintenance

Maintain the vehicle according to the manufacturer's schedule, which is found in the owner's manual. It will help your vehicle last longer and save money in repairs in the long run. Some vehicles have codes that display for the driver when needed maintenance is due – such as 'A1' or 'B3'. The maintenance needed by the code is also described in the owner's manual. You can also find this information performing an online search, with the vehicle's year, make and model, such as "2015 Toyota Highlander Maintenance Schedule". Do not necessarily pay for all the "recommended" maintenance at the dealership or another mechanic. Many dealerships or other mechanics suggest more frequent servicing, or fluid changes, or add items that are not necessary for maintenance when a vehicle is brought in for service. Simply follow the service schedule recommended by the manufacturer.

Since vehicles lose about half their value every four years or so, one of the smartest things you can do is keep each car, truck or SUV a long time. I recommend keeping each one for a minimum of ten years. This way, you will have a paid-off vehicle for many years and get most of the usable life out of it before buying another one.

Action Items for vehicle purchases:
1) **Do your homework in terms of dealer cost of a new car.**
2) **Know the trade-in value of your existing vehicle.**
3) **Get a quote from more than one dealer.**
4) **Be willing to walk away from a bad deal.**

5) **Do not succumb to expensive offerings in the finance department.**
6) **Update your auto insurance with the new vehicle on your policy.**
7) **Use the maintenance schedule recommended by the vehicle manufacturer – not the dealership or other party.**
8) **Keep each vehicle a minimum of ten years.**

Chapter 20

How Do I Get A Good Job?

Following a financial roadmap out of college implicitly assumes that there is earned income with which to plan. Most people go to college in hopes that their degrees in their respective fields will put them in the position of earning more money over their lifetimes. However, I have found that many college students do not know how to go about getting that first real job after they graduate.

Here are some ideas. Network with others. Build relationships with people that you know. Be genuine. Remember that the people you go to school with may be important to your success later. I had a student in a negotiations class who systematically lied in negotiations simulations with fellow students to try to get a better grade. Other students found out about this both during post-negotiation debriefings, as well as student discussions out of class. For the rest of the course, no one trusted him and he suffered in his negotiations with fellow students. One of the things I pointed out to the class is that the way you and I treat others can have much broader implications than just a grade in a college course. I would imagine that even 20 years from now those students who were misled by their fellow student will have a hard time trusting him.

Below are the Action Items for seeking and getting a job:
1. If you live near your alma mater, **go to the Career Placement Center** of the university you currently attend or from which you graduated. Make an appointment to meet the director. Find out what resources are there.
2. Utilizing some of the steps below, **practice interviewing** there. **Watch a recorded mock interview of yourself**, if the Center has those resources.

Many shortcomings can be identified and addressed in these videos, such as appearing nervous, talking too fast, speaking too long, etc. Most people vastly underutilize the career placement centers at their schools. One of the things I tell my students is to **work as hard to get a job as you would in the job.** This means it takes hours of preparation, planning and practice. It also means taking the time to research the entities or companies with whom you might interview. One of the most common questions in interviews is, "Why do you want to work for us?" You need to demonstrate some of specific knowledge of the company or people there when answering this question. This lets the interviewer know that you cared enough to do that research, and that you are motivated.

3. **Have a one-page resume that is perfect** and ready to hand to recruiters. The resume should never be more than one page. It should simply be a summary of your academic and work experience and achievements or awards. A person should be able to glance at it and within 30 seconds know what they want to know about you. This means your name and contact information should be bold. It also means the font on the resume should be large enough to be easy to read. Your degree and major should be quickly and easily identifiable, and if you have done well in school, your grade point average or class rank should be prominent. Consider having the career placement center at your university help you write and/or proofread your resume.

4. **Practice and be ready to answer the top 100 interview questions most likely to be asked.** Search the internet for the top 100 interview questions. Have specific, short answers ready for an interviewer. Most interviews last less than 30 minutes and you are competing with everyone else being interviewed. It is important to be prepared and to make a good impression; answers should be shorter than two minutes. For example, if an interviewer says, "Tell me about yourself," he or she is not really looking to hear your life story. They are looking to hear how you might be a good fit for the company. So within those two minutes, tell them how you got interested in your major and how you would like to use it to benefit the company and others. Respond honestly and thoughtfully. At the end of an interview, smile, and thank interviewer for his or her time. Shake their hand firmly but not too hard, and express your genuine interest in working for them and their company. Also ask for a business card. Immediately after the interview, send the interviewer a <u>handwritten</u> thank you note. People remember these actions because

they are rare. Thank you notes also convey that you are motivated, thoughtful and polite.

5. If you are not already employed in your chosen field, **attend job fairs.** Find out about job opportunities and fairs from the career placement center at the university from which you graduated. Have the resume ready to hand to recruiters at the job fair. **Always dress professionally** when attending job fairs and interviews. This means a coat and tie for men and professional suits or professionally looking dresses for women. It means looking your very best in terms of personal appearance. At the risk of sounding too much like a parent, check your teeth and breath. At the job fair, **schedule as many interviews as you reasonably can.** It takes practice to become a good interviewee. Many people also find that they develop an interest in a company during interview they did not realize they would have.

6. If and when you are offered a position, **negotiate the highest salary and benefits you can.** This sounds so basic. But many students and recent graduates do not know how to put themselves in the best position to earn the highest salary possible. In my negotiations course, I discuss the advantages of alternative options. This means in a job search, try to secure more than one job offer. This adds to your negotiating leverage when discussing salary and benefits, since you can potentially consider both offers and discuss the possibilities with employers interested in hiring you. Realize that even a 4% or 5% increase in initial salary will likely flow through in future years, as raises and promotions are usually based on starting salary. Thus, this higher starting salary can potentially result in well over $100,000 of additional income over a working career.

Action Items:
1) **Go to the Career Placement Center of your university.**
2) **Have perfect one page resume available.**
3) **Be prepared to answer commonly asked interview questions.**
4) **Attend Job Fairs. Dress professionally for them.**
5) **Schedule as many interviews as possible.**
6) **Negotiate the highest salary you can, when offered a position.**
7) **When you are offered a job, celebrate!**

PART VI: THE YEARS AHEAD

Chapter 21

Future Steps Forward

T he most important thing about this book is for you to <u>implement</u> the ideas
in it and follow through. This includes the following steps:

1) **Review and revise your goals and finances each year.** Life is constantly
   changing. Jobs change, incomes change, investments change, tax laws
   change, your goals may change, the number of people in the home may
   change, job benefits may change, etc. It is vital to review your financial
   plan in light of these and other possible changes, and also to see how well
   goals are being met and realized. Choose a time of year that is less busy
   for you to review your goals and plans. Many times, the end of the year
   is not a good time, as Christmas and New Year's are often times spent
   with family or on vacation. So, choose a day each year that is slower so
   that you can thoughtfully review your financial progress, and adjust goals
   as needed. Unfortunately, most people do not follow through with their
   financial plan after it has been created. Instead, most forget about it. Do
   not be one of those persons! As I have pointed out in this book, **financial
   success is as much about discipline as it is about money.**

2) Use the benchmarks at the end of this chapter as guides regarding how
   much debt you have at various ages. The table below lists debt compared to income. When people are young, they take on a lot of debt due
   to mortgages, student loans, replacing cars, etc. Over the years, the debt
   should go down both in dollar terms, as well as in comparison to income.
   Here is an example how to use the table below to track your debt compared to your income at various ages. If you had total debts, including a

mortgage, student loans and a car loan of $160,000 and an annual gross income of $80,000 your Debt-to-Income Ratio would be: $160,000 / $80,000 = 2.00. That ratio should decline as income rises and debts are paid off over the years.

3) The table below also provides a guide regarding the percentage of <u>gross</u> income you should be saving for retirement savings in the years ahead. Here is an example using the table below regarding retirement savings at various ages: When you are 30 years old, you should be saving 20% of your gross income towards retirement. This is not easy and is certainly above the national average. But it is doable. The ratio at each age includes all the money you are saving for retirement in any IRA or 401(k) or 403(b) account. It also includes any employer match that may be available. If you do not have a 401(k) or 403(b) plan available, save in an IRA first (I recommend a Roth IRA), then put the rest of your retirement savings into a brokerage account. You can save large amounts of income by growing the percentage of salary that you save each year. The way to do this is to put about half of any raise you get at work towards your retirement savings. So, if you get a 4% raise, add 2% to the amount you are saving for retirement.

Below are the suggested ratios for the maximum Debt-to-Income Ratio at various ages, and minimum amount of your gross income you should save each year for retirement.

Age	Maximum Debt-to-Income Ratio	Minimum Percentage of Gross Income You Should Save At Each Age For Retirement
25	2.00	10%
26	1.95	12%
27	1.90	14%
28	1.85	16%
29	1.80	18%
30	1.75	20%
35	1.50	25%
40	1.25	25%
45	1.00	25%
50	0.75	25%
55	0.50	25%
60	0.25	25%
65	0.00	25%

If you use these ratios as a guide, you can have success in paying down debt, and building up wealth for your retirement, and for the future of your children, and their children. **If you cannot achieve these ratios at the corresponding age, do not be discouraged! Keep saving more for retirement and pay off debt each year.** These are only guidelines.

4) **Track your Net Worth at least once a year. Here is the formula:** Net worth is the current value of all of your assets, minus the current value of all of your debts. Current value for physical items, such as a home or car is what something you own would sell for today in the case of assets. In regards to debts, current value is how much you owe today. Your assets include all of your savings accounts, brokerage accounts, retirement accounts, etc. Assets also include the current value of your home and your vehicles. Add them all up, to get Total Assets. Note that the current value of clothes and furniture is likely to be very low, as these items lose most of their value after they are purchased. So, assign a low value to them. Debts include the current amounts owed on a home mortgage, car loans, student loans, credit card debt that is not paid off each month, and any other debt you might have. Add all of these up to get Total Debts. Total Debts are subtracted from the total value of your assets. Your goal overall should be for your net worth to rise each year. That happens as your assets, through savings and appreciation, grow over time, and your debts decrease over time.

Saving money and paying off debt is not easy, but it is a self-less act. By following the guides in this book and using these ratios through the years, you can have financial success for you, and your family. I would like to close this chapter quoting a Proverb. Of course, this verse applies to both men and women today. Proverbs 13:22. "A good man leaves an inheritance to his children's children."

Action Items:
1) **Review and revise your financial goals at least once a year.**
2) **Use the benchmarks in this chapter as guides towards debt reduction at different ages.**
3) **Use the benchmarks in this chapter as guides towards the amount of gross salary you should save each year for retirement through the years.**
4) **Track your Net Worth each year.**

Final Thoughts

I hope you have found this book easy to read and understand. I hope the Action Items will benefit you not just in the next month or two, but for the rest of your life. As a father, a professor, and as a Christian, I have told our daughters and my students that if there is a mission statement for my life, it is, "The Next Generation Is the Most Important One." I believe that with everything I am. My goal is to serve Almighty God by investing in your life with the information in this book! I hope and pray that the investment of time that you have made in reading it will make a remarkable difference in your future. Most of all, I hope your life is improved after reading it. My goal is to help people succeed after college. It is a joy to invest in the next generation as a father, professor, and now as an author.

Sincerely, Dr. Andrew Schaffer

Appendix

(Recommended Web Sites)

Budgeting:
   www.Mint.com
   www.youneedabudget.com

Competitive Interest Rates in Bank Accounts and on Loans:
   www.bankrate.com

Credit Reports:
   www.annualcreditreport.com

Credit Scores:
   www.creditkarma.com

Disability Insurance:
   www.amica.com
   www.nm.com

FDIC Insurance on bank accounts:
   https://www.fdic.gov/deposit/covered/categories.html.

Health Insurance:
   www.ehealthinsurance.com

Investments:
    www.betterment.com
    www.Fidelity.com
    www.vanguard.com

Life Insurance:
    www.amica.com
    www.nm.com
    www.usaa.com

Online Mortgage Calculator: 30-year loan:
http://www.dynamicontent.net/dcv2/indiv_calc.php?calc=1&key=wolfecpa2

Online Mortgage Calculator: 15-year
http://www.dynamicontent.net/dcv2/indiv_calc.php?calc=6&key=wolfecpa2

Personal Financial Planning Links:
    www.Kiplinger.com
    www.Money.com

Tax Software:
    https://turbotax.intuit.com/

Vehicle Information Site:
    www.edmunds.com
    www.kbb.com
    www.truecar.com

Vehicle Purchase Calculator:
http://www.dynamicontent.net/dcv2/indiv_calc.php?calc=21&key=wolfecpa2

Vehicle Pre-Negotiated Purchase Prices:
    www.USAA.com

Web Link:
    Facebook.com/financialplanning4grads